UNDERSTANDING MILITARY TECHNOLOGY

2,50

UNDERSTANDING
MILITARY
TECHNOLOGY

HAMLYN

Published by the
Hamlyn Publishing Group Limited
Bridge House, Twickenham
Middlesex, England

This book was designed and produced by
Campbell Rawkins Limited, 2 Barbon Close,
London, WC1.

Designer: Bob Gordon

Diagrams by: David Ashby
Picture Research by: The Research House

Production Consultant: ALMAC (Book
Production Services Ltd.
Filmset by: Colset Private Ltd, Singapore
Reproduction by: Dot Gradations, Essex, England
Printed by Graficromo s.a., Cordoba, Spain

ISBN 0 600 50032 2

Contents

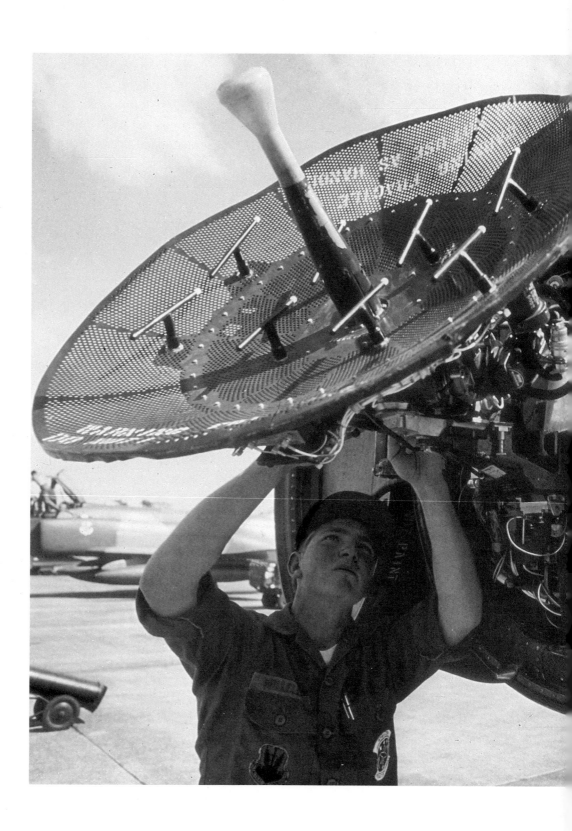

Introduction

Every year the US Department of Defense publishes a booklet called *Soviet Military Power* laying out in some detail what US intelligence departments know about their superpower opponent. Several of its observations are included in this book.

It's not just a matter of counting divisions, tanks, warships, missiles and so on — more and more it concentrates on the state of Soviet weapon science. One veteran US commentator likened it to the Coca Cola Corporation putting out a statement about 'how great tasting Pepsi was' and in a sense, that is its purpose, to light a fire under Congress to further loosen the pursestrings on America's own massive investment in military technology.

The irony is that the strategy of nuclear deterrence strives to ensure its own futility, to ensure that weapons of mass destruction are never used. But the conflict is there and is pursued with a passion, consuming budgets greater than that of actual wars past. The conflict is fought in the laboratories and testing grounds, showing up years later as actual hardware, giving politicans choices which they might never have brought upon themselves in the first place. The Strategic Defense Initiative or 'Star Wars' is a classic example. Because the scientists say it can be done the temptation to try it out is overwhelming, anyway the Russians are doing it aren't they? The results of SDI research meanwhile may drastically change the pattern of superpower relationships with a leap into the strategic unknown and dominate the closing years of the 20th Century.

Military technology is always wrapped in secrecy but the need to understand it is greater than ever before, for the policy makers who must turn armed force into practical military tools as much as for ordinary people who pay for it with their taxes and live every day under its threat. The purpose of this book is to make that understanding easier.

1 COMPUTERS: THE NEW MILITARY FORCE

Military people have their own language, a 'Milspeak', which distils complex concepts into a short burst of letters and numbers. They use phrases like C-cubed I, AI, DEEC, CSAS and PGSM the way most people talk about the weather. Between two people who understand the jargon such communication is highly efficient. As far as the non-initiate is concerned, it generates a sort of high-pitched droning between the ears. Simply translating the acronym into plain language, though, merely proves that Milspeak is not just a conspiracy to keep the public out of military detail. It is necessary: just try working the phrase 'command, control, communications and intelligence' into any sort of meaningful sentence which can be comprehended on the first pass.

Milspeak reaches its highest levels in the newest of military technologies: the use of electronic data processing in warfare. The impact of the computer on daily life has been large enough; in warfare, which was already the most technology-dominated of human activities, the implications of new computer technology are so vast that it is difficult to comprehend them.

The relationship between computers and the military has see-sawed over the years. Military requirements, specifically the need to crack machine-generated codes, brought the mathematical thinkers of the 1930s together with the electrical engineers and led to the creation of the first electronic computers. After 1945 military sponsorship of computing continued, but on a defined track: the military people were interested in developing computers to do certain tasks, such as navigating a missile or directing hundreds of fighters to their targets. The same 'goal-directed' approach characterised NASA's extensive sponsorship of early work in micro-electronics, which was directed at producing very light automatic control systems for spacecraft. The question was always 'Can a computer do task X?' rather than 'What can a computer, of Y power, do for the science of warfare?'

The great computer explosion changed that attitude for ever. It was based on micro-electronics, but used as NASA and the US Air Force had never expected. The critical discovery was that, as the new microprocessor 'chips' became smaller, they became simultaneously faster, easier to produce in quantity, and cheaper. The result was a boom which totally outpaced the adaptability of the services and the defence contractors, and left most in-production weapon systems looking, at least in the eyes of the computer specialist, hopelessly archaic.

There are now two responding trends under way. The first is the incorporation of current electronic technology into military systems; the second is the services' resumption of their position as the leading sponsors of highly advanced electronic technologies. Combined with the military's new and more open attitude to computing, the latter points to some remarkable advances between now and the year 2000.

There are two main avenues of development, both regarded as 'strategic technologies'. One is the design and, eventually, mass production of micro-electronic components of ever smaller size, packing more and more processing power into a given space. The technology behind the new 'superchips' is generally known as very large-scale integration (VLSI); in US military circles, it is commonly described as very high-speed integrated circuitry (VHSIC, pronounced 'vizzic') because that is the name of the specific Pentagon programme involved.

The other aim of government-sponsored research is the creation of 'supercomputers' or 'fifth-generation computers', incredibly

Computers have come to dominate the high technology battlefield at every level of application. The French infantryman below is using a digital message pad, part of the Thomson-CSF Field data terminal TRC 743. At the other end of the spectrum the Cray-1 computer (right) has massive number crunching power, able to decipher from the cacophony of the oceans the sonar trace of a distant submarine or predict the flight path through space of an intercontinental ballistic missile

powerful data-processors. They will use VLSI technology, but will call for other advances in computer engineering to achieve their enormous speeds. At times, the limiting factor may be that the electronic impulses can travel no faster than light on their way from one part of the computer to another. Such speeds are beyond current experience; theory gives some ideas of what such a computer will do, but nobody can be absolutely certain. The hope of computer science, though, is that the new machines will be able to think in a new way, and use data in the same manner as the human mind. The goal is 'artificial intelligence' (AI) — the step from number-crunching to intuition.

AI is a broad and variously defined term. An AI system, however, will have certain characteristics. It will make decisions based on patterns of data, and on partial data. It will be capable of responding in a certain way to a pattern of data that resembles another previously learned pattern, even if the individual data points are different: this is sometimes called an 'expert' or 'knowledge-based' system. It will be capable of setting priorities for its actions — the B-1's electronic countermeasures system already does this, concentrating its power on the most imminent threat — but it will also be able to set priorities for its own internal processing. This 'scheduling' ability is tremendously important, because it allows the system to bring all its power to bear on a single problem. Whether the new fifth-generation computers will pass the classic test for intelligence — the ability to

respond to any question in a manner which is humanly indistinguishable from the response of a human mind — is a matter for debate, but they will certainly allow researchers to change the way all computers think, including smaller VLSI-based devices.

The impact of AI on the military scene is also impossible to assess with any pretension to accuracy, but to look at the way in which current technology is being used, or could be used in a few years, is to gain some idea of the degree to which military technology is becoming intertwined with the technology of information. This process is well under way, but is not happening overnight for a number of good reasons. One is that the application of computing to a multi-faceted, advanced industry such as defence leaves almost no part of it unaffected. There is virtually nothing in the industry which cannot be significantly improved by smarter systems of automated control, and it takes both time and money to research and develop advances in so many areas and then implement them as production programmes.

Computing, too, has always been an innovative industry, and shows nothing like the same countervailing conservatism as, for example, is found in aerospace. In computer development, the result of a gross error in programming may be a 'crash', but all that means is that the computer will not operate until a suitably modified duplicate of the original program is written and run. An error of the same type, or even a simple oversight, in the program for a flight control system could

destroy an irreplaceable prototype or, at worst, kill a pilot. The same applies to the control of a warship's defensive systems.

Making such critical computer systems acceptable for military use is not just a matter of designing a system that is reliable. One of the biggest tasks in developing a mission-critical computer program is defining the degree of reliability needed, and then design-ing tests to prove that those standards have been met. The ease of making repairs and modifications, called 'patches', to a computer program has, until now, obviated the need for 'fail-safe' or 'fail-operative' design in software. In the words of a conventional engineer's cynical adage: 'If architects built houses the way programmers write software, one wood-pecker could cause the collapse of civilisation'.

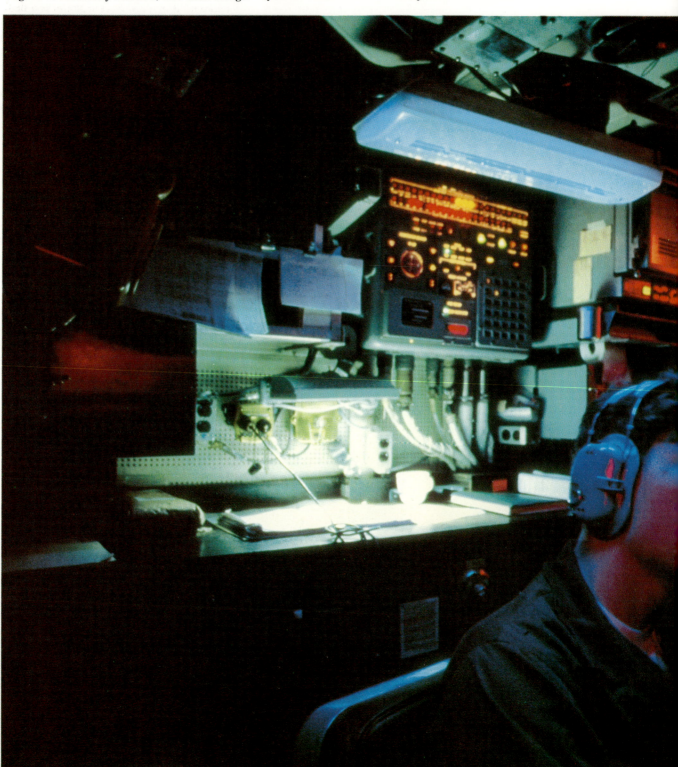

A nuclear powered submarine is dependent on computer power to make it function. This is the sonar operator's station aboard one of the newest US Navy nuclear powered attack submarines

The development of commercial computers also bypassed the issue of ruggedness and resistance to the environment. As anyone knows who has worked with computers, they can be temperamental beasts, easily upset by even a slight variation in room temperature. This was one of the problems that was accepted in the course of the computer boom, but is unacceptable for military use. It is pos-

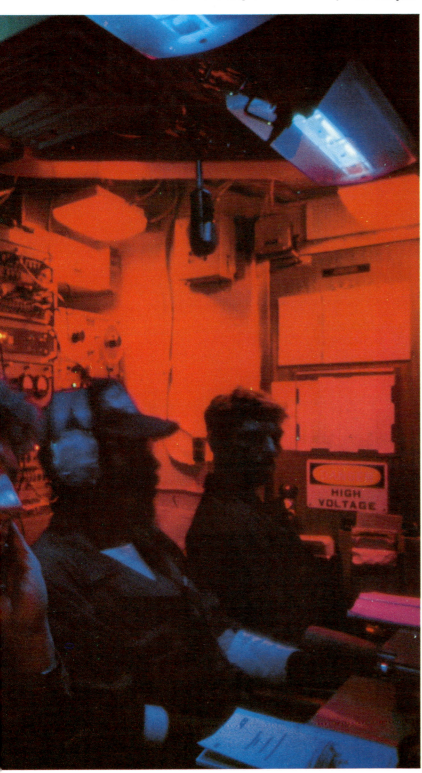

sible to take a commercial computer, and seal it into a rugged container with shock and climatic protection, but the result is a heavier and less reliable system than a properly designed military computer.

Another important factor is the protection of the computer against electromagnetic pulse (EMP) effects from lightning or nuclear blast. Part of the reason for the close military involvement in VLSI development is a desire to ensure that EMP resistance is taken into account in the design of the basic building blocks from which future systems will be made. In that way, it is hoped, it should become easier to protect the entire system.

Security is a major design consideration. Commercial computers had been working for many years before it was found that they leaked information, in the form of radio-frequency emissions, like sieves or Washington sources. Only in the past couple of years, in fact, has the US Department of Defense arrived at its Tempest standards for computer and terminal security.

Another reason for the apparent backwardness of the defence community is that the commercial computer boom was the result of fierce competition among different companies, each with their different operating systems. But to the military user, interoperability is more important than sheer performance. The task of developing suitable and acceptable standards for military computer systems, without placing heavy constraints on the computer developers, has been a major one.

Contemporary computer technology is now being applied to many military systems. Perhaps the most important of all concerns the most basic element of military operations: command. The phrase 'command, communications, control and intelligence' deserves to be spelt out and considered before substituting the standard, computer-age shorthand C^3I. In fact, it sums up what went right for Napoleon, on his better days, and most of what went wrong at Balaclava. From the point of view of the lay observer, the trouble with C^3I technology is that the field is so large that it is hard to comprehend it all.

The application of computers to C^3I goes back to the creation of the first 'automated ground environments' for defence against bombers in the 1950s. Essentially, the role of automation was not to take decisions, but to provide the human commanders with processed information on outside activity — for example, the speed and heading of a radar target, and whether or not it could be confirmed as friendly — and to communicate the commanders' orders to the fighter in the air.

The next major application of C^3I systems

was to warships. A modern warship is no longer commanded routinely from the bridge, but from a dark, enclosed tactical control centre where screens display targets in the air, on the surface and underwater. Perhaps there is no better indication of the importance of C^{3}I in naval warfare than the fact that the US Navy's latest class of surface combatant was for many years simply named Aegis, after its C^{3}I system.

Automated C^{3}I made its first appearance in land-based systems and ships, for the simple reason that the computers of the day were too large to fit anywhere else. Another limitation in those early days was that C^{3}I systems had to be large and self-sufficient, partly because computers were too big and costly to be deployed in large numbers, but mainly because there was no way of transmitting large quantities of data between one station and another. Both these limitations have been removed by modern computer technology which accounts for the steadily increasing importance of C^{3}I in defence budgets.

Technically, it is now feasible for a unit of almost any size to be 'on-line' with a C^{3}I system. A terminal weighing around ten pounds, with entirely adequate power to format and transmit useful information, and meeting Tempest security specifications, not only exists but is on the open market. As for communications, message-switching and digital transmission technology has increased the capacity of satellite links to a vast degree, making it possible for the systems to be opened up to more users.

Some of the major C^{3}I programmes now under way include the joint tactical information distribution system (JTIDS), which is designed to provide the latest data on enemy units to terminals on fighter aircraft and vehicles. There is GPS/Navstar, the satellite-based global positioning system which allows fighter pilots or artillery commanders to fix their positions with almost unearthly precision. PLSS, the precision location strike system, uses airborne receivers mounted in a trio of high-flying TR-1s, combined with a

ground station, to fix the position of hostile radars with sufficient accuracy for a rocket or artillery attack. Information technology, or the use of computers to process data and communicate it at high speed, makes all these systems possible.

As is the case with all information systems, the aim with C³I is to get the right amount of information — not too little, but certainly not too much — to the right place. A modern fighting unit has enough C³I sensors and sensor platforms at its disposal to gather an immense amount of information. These include electronic/communications intelligence aircraft, airborne and surface-based radars and the passive electronic surveillance devices installed on almost all its combat aircraft. But it also has a direct link to the military communications satellite system, and thus to the entire signals intelligence (Sigint) and reconnaissance machine.

But is this entirely a good thing? Given current technology, there is enough information available to swamp the entire decision-

making process in a sea of data. The commander is faced with a difficult decision: when to stop acquiring information and make a move.

The same human-factors issue can arise at any level and can certainly do so in the case of the single-seat fighter pilot, who is busy enough flying the aircraft. On top of that, the pilot may have JTIDS data, and information from the ever more sophisticated passive electronic surveillance measures (ESM) aboard the aircraft. The problem is the same: technology can provide more information than can be used.

It is at this point that the potential for 'intelligent' computers begins to emerge. If C³I systems can be made to carry out much more sophisticated analyses of incoming information — the sort that can at present only be done by human analysts at human speed — the potential for gathering more raw data and making real use of it is there. But the crunch could come in two words: 'proven reliability'. How do you ensure that human fallibility has not planted a certain association in the AI system, an association that leads to the wrong conclusion? And worse, how do you prove that the system is free of such problems? After all, many of history's great military blunders were made in full knowledge of the facts. If it is possible to create artificial intelligence, it is certainly conceivable that a design error could create artificial stupidity.

There is one realm of C³I in which immense computer power, and probably elements of AI as well, will be not only desirable but essential: the control of a space-based defence system. If such a system is to work, the decision to fire must be made literally within seconds of the first missile leaving the silos. Otherwise, the attacker can be confident that many of his boosters will soar serenely through the first and most important line of defence, the only line in which every good hit takes out ten or more warheads, and will fire his heavy-payload missiles first. There is simply no time for a human decision but, as in the case of any attack, the first warning will not be unambiguous. The first launch will register on the defence system's staring infra-red (IR) arrays — but is it a missile launch or an explosion? An ICBM or a space probe? An attack or a test? A wrong call may not start a nuclear war — advocates of such a defence system claim that a misfire would be no worse than a meteor shower — but would certainly leave the system badly depleted. If the judgement capacity of the system were not far beyond the capability of any computer system conceived to date, a deliberate false alarm could be a very effective option for an enemy.

The use of current information technology and future ventures into AI in the world of C³I represent the 'macro' end of military computing. However, almost any military system will reflect the impact of computer technology in the coming years, and none will do so more than aerospace weapons. Despite being on the leading edge of technology, aerospace is only now catching up with the computer world. The reaon for this is that the aerospace industry based most of its early automatic control systems on analogue technology. In an analogue electronic system, changing voltages act as 'analogues' or models of whatever quantity is being controlled or measured: the attitude of the aircraft, the opening or closing of a control valve, or the position of a control surface.

The computer revolution, however, was based on 'digital' systems in which quantities were represented by numbers rather than voltages. The development of the microprocessor chip, a purely digital technology, has meant that a digital system can carry out far more than an analogue system of the same size, permitting new functions to be built in. Its performance can be steadily improved in the light of experience by improving the 'software', or the instructions which set out the relationship between the quantities outside and the numbers which represent them. Digital systems can exchange information more easily than analogue systems, allowing them to work closely together. Microprocessors have proven to be extremely reliable, and, moreover, the power of a digital system makes it possible to add a great deal of built-in testing power. Most digital systems in use or under development today have maintenance modes in which they will find and display any malfunctions, contributing to an enormous reduction in maintenance costs compared with analogue devices.

These and other advantages made the transition to digital technology inevitable, and it is a challenge both to aerospace and computing people. Digital computing is now being used to perform 'flight-critical' functions which may be entirely impossible with analogue equipment and, in engineering terminology, 'flight-critical' refers to a situation in which a failure does not leave a safe platform for pilot ejection.

An example of this technology, now being demonstrated for potential application to aircraft such as the US Air Force's Advanced Tactical Fighter (ATF), is the Honeywell digital flight control system (DFCS) on the Grumman X-29A fighter technology demonstrator. Designed for high efficiency at high speed, the X-29A is unstable at low speeds: if it is disturbed from its flight path its natural tendency is to continue moving away from its original attitude. The DFCS software, rather than any mechanical or electrical device, defines what movements of the control surfaces take place when the pilot moves the control stick, taking into account the aircraft's attitude, altitude and airspeed.

The writing and validation of the DFCS software has been the biggest single task in the X-29A programme, more demanding even than the design of the wing. It has involved estimating the response of the aircraft over its entire performance envelope, together with the effectiveness of its control systems, and ensuring that the controls will move to give a constant and predictable control response in the cockpit. The same mathematical model of the aircraft is used in a simulator, together with flight-qualified DFCS hardware, to provide some hands-on experience before the first flight.

Some important questions have to be answered in the process. It is one thing to make an aircraft fly in a stable manner, and

Left: *The main computer at NORAD, North American Aerospace Defence Command, receiving and processing information from a global network of sensors*

Below: *At the heart of the US Navy's Aegis fleet air defence system are four AN/UYK-7 digital computers which are designed to handle the massive battle management loads of directing missile defence against multiple targets*

another to make it simultaneously stable and responsive. Also, with a control system as powerful as that of the X-29A the designers must judge the points at which the flight envelope should be restricted, balancing the need to maintain flight safety with the requirement to extract the maximum possible performance from the aircraft.

Developing a digital system is a very different task from the development of a traditional analogue flight control system because of the ease with which the software can be changed. The X-29A, for instance, will be flown with a DFCS program designed to err on the side of safety. Should the designers decide, at a later stage, that more or less response is required in a given flight regime, the necessary 'patch' can be tested on the simulator and then added to the operational DFCS simply by running a different tape before flight. While the ability to change the characteristics of the flight control system without physical modification is a major advantage of digital technology, it means adding the whole new task of software updating to the development programme.

Another aspect of digital systems, which likewise is both a challenge and an opportunity, is the degree to which different components can work together. Most defence authorities are developing high-order computer languages for common use on all military computers, and these provide the basis for levels of integration which are quite unattainable with analogue computing. The usual means of communication between digital subsystems on board an aircraft, ship or tank is called a 'bus', and gets its name from the fact that it is a single route connecting all

the systems. The 'passengers' on the bus are packages of electronic information, each with a special code that identifies its destination. A bus, which physically consists of a single cable, allows any system to talk to any or all of the others, and can thus replace a vast number of individual circuits. As in the case of languages, national and international standards for defence-system buses are being established.

A remarkable air combat over New Mexico in August 1982 showed some of the immense potential of integrated systems. The protagonists were a mechanically-unmodified F-15B Eagle and a PQM-102, a remotely-piloted modification of a Delta Dagger interceptor. The drone, over three miles ahead of the F-15, initiated the engagement by pulling a 4 *g* turn. Normally, the F-15 pilot would have followed the quarry through the turn, trying to close on its tail, but instead he pulled an immediate, shallower turn at higher speed. As the drone pulled through 90 degrees of its turn, the F-15 was approaching in its 'ten o'clock' position, that is to say not quite head-on, at a relative speed between 760 and 810 knots. Both aircraft were still turning as the F-15 pilot fired his 20 mm M61 cannon at a range of just over a mile, in a 1·7-second,

Far Left: *Computer power is bringing about a transformation in the very shape of combat aircraft. Computers can 'fly' an artificially unstable aircraft, a so-called 'controlled configuration vehicle', automatically performing flight corrections hundreds of times per second. This is Mitsubishi's T2 prototype CCV*

Below: *An even more dramatic new shape in the sky is the Grumman X-29A forward swept wing technology demonstrator. Writing the software for the digital flight control system was the biggest technical challenge of the programme*

171-shell burst. It should have taken a jet-age von Richthofen to score a single hit against a manoeuvring, high-deflection target, but from what little was left of the PQM-102 it was concluded that it had taken 30 strikes before coming apart.

What was significant was that the F-15, its gun, its sensors and its flight control system were all standard. The only modification to the F-15 was the installation of a package of new controls and software called Integrated Flight/Fire Control (IFFC) or Firefly, which allowed the radar to 'talk' to the flight control system. The fire-control system tracked the target and the predicted trajectory of the shells and passed 'error signals' to the flight control system. The pilot used the controls for coarse tracking of the target, but the fine pointing of the aircraft was carried out using IFFC. Even the programme managers had not originally expected such effects. At the start of the programme it was believed that the radar itself would not be accurate enough for automated air-to-air gunnery, and it was planned to fit a tv-type tracker to the F-15. The switch to the radar was made only because the tv hardware proved unreliable.

The Firefly programme has shown what can be done in the air-to-air arena by integrating existing systems with improved software. Another USAF development, based on a modified F-16, is extending the same principle to air-to-ground weapon delivery. Such integration programmes are only a foretaste of what is technically feasible for new-generation military aircraft, and of what is required for such types as the Advanced Tactical Fighter. Even a brief description of the avionic system aboard ATF gives some idea of the degree to which computer technology will affect aircraft and weapon design.

Perhaps surprisingly, ATF will have no central 'master computer' co-ordinating and supporting the entire system. Such a configuration, 'centralised architecture' in avionics terminology, was necessary on some early airborne digital systems, when an aircraft could only accommodate one powerful digital computer. Now that computer power is cheap and compact, it makes more sense to design 'distributed architecture' providing each system with all the processing and memory that it needs. The radar, for instance, can be fitted with a digital 'signal processor' which analyses the raw radar returns and delivers refined data directly to the cockpit display. In-service centralised digital systems such as the US Navy's A-New anti-submarine warfare system (fitted to the P-3C Orion) are gradually evolving into distributed layouts as new, smarter subsystems are retrofitted into the fleet.

The links between the various systems will not necessarily be purely electronic. A major consideration in the design of military avionic systems will be electromagnetic pulse (EMP): lightning strikes or, more significantly, nuclear flash. EMP can cause serious failures in digital systems unless they are insulated and the pulse is channelled around them. Protecting individual control units is not too difficult, but shielding long electrical cables adds weight and complexity, and they are still the weakest point in the system. A strong alternative is optical links, in which signals are converted to light pulses and transmitted along fibre-optic cables. These could be used for

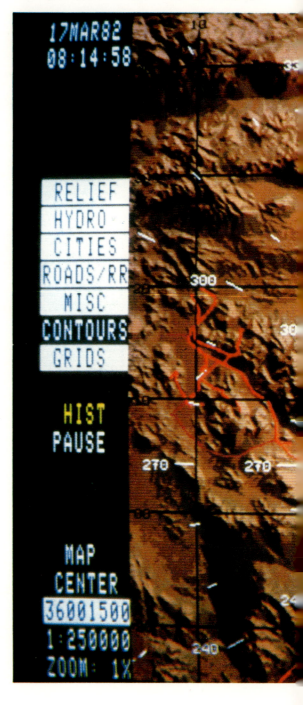

Computer power has another military function — in creating combat environments without moving from a training simulator. The USAF's Magic simulator (**right**) allows tactical air-to-ground missions to be flown in relative earthbound comfort. The computerised wargame (**below**) allows constant playing and replaying of different 'scenarios' to refine tactics and technology

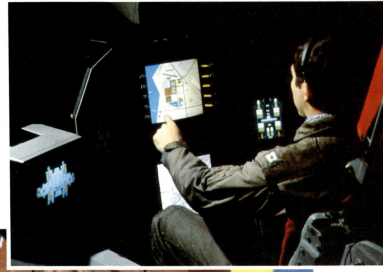

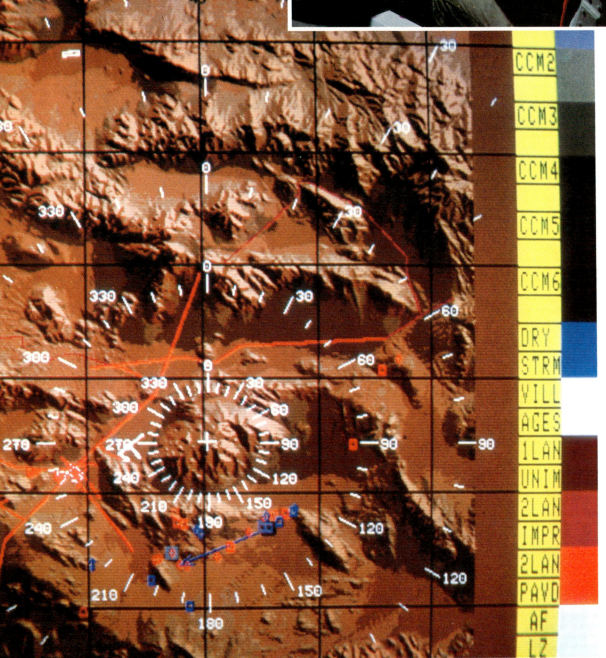

data buses or to signal flight controls — a 'fly-by-light' or 'fly-by-optics' system.

The main electronic control systems on board ATF will all be digital. They will include the engine and flight controls, the fire-control system and navigation equipment, and systems to generate the symbology projected on the pilot's head-up display system. The aircraft itself may feature a variable-camber, mission-adaptive wing (MAW), used to reduce drag, increase manoeuvring ability and tighten turns. Its engines will have vectoring and reversing nozzles, primarily to shorten the runway requirement but also used for pitch control and braking. Both will be under automatic control by the digital flight and engine control systems.

Another intriguing possibility is that digital control systems may be able to adapt to failure or damage, getting the best performance possible from a damaged engine, auto-matically compensating for asymmetric power or modifying control commands to reflect reduced hydraulic pressure. Such 'adaptive' control systems could allow more missions to be completed, and would certainly ease the piloting task.

Other 'stops' on the ATF data bus will include its electronic warfare system, including both passive (listening and pinpointing) and active (jamming and deceiving) devices. It will be sufficiently powerful to provide useful information to the fire-control system, cutting down on tell-tale active radar transmissions. It will draw information from the navigation system, for instance by using groundspeed and course data and taking two bearings on a static radar, it will be able to fix its position and, possibly, pass the information down the bus to a defensive anti-radar missile.

Tactical control systems on ships are likely to evolve in the same way, although they are concerned mainly with the control of weapons: ship manoeuvres are less complex. However, ships may be the first systems to revert to a new kind of centralised architecture in which a central, intelligent processor is available to assist the individual digital systems.

Supercomputers will contribute to defence programmes in other ways. One of the most important could be the development of what is called a numerical aerodynamic simulator (NAS), or, in plain language, an electronic wind tunnel. Such machines will be able to predict and map the air-flow around a complete aircraft, like a wind tunnel. But the NAS will be able to test computer 'models' at full scale, at speeds far higher than Ames' own full-scale wind tunnel. Unlike physical wind-tunnel models, which can cost millions of dollars, these computer models can be easily modified to reflect design changes or alternatives. The NAS requires immense computer power, in the 'gigaflop' range: that is to say, the machine must be able to handle one billion floating-point calculations every second.

Aerodynamicists believe that such a device could be of immense help in developing the hypersonic airframes and supersonic-combustion ramjet engines of the next-generation spaceplane, the trans-atmospheric vehicle (TAV), and other advanced aircraft.

Now emerging as a military technology of great importance for the coming decades is robotics, the branch of engineering which couples basic artificial intelligence to the ability to take physical action. Experimenters in robotics have created machines which can operate in a much more sophisticated manner, sensing and responding to the unexpected, negotiating obstacles to reach a given goal, and updating their memories according to experience. So far, though, such machines

The Mission Adaptive Wing (MAW) has no hinges, flaps or spoilers to break the smooth contours of its upper surface. The flight control computer constantly adapts the wing to the optimum configuration for particular flight conditions while strong but flexible composite materials make the technology possible

work on a 'stop-think-move' cycle because the capacity of a small computer is inadequate to match a constant speed of motion. In the next few years a team of US Navy researchers hopes to have modified an armoured vehicle so that it can follow another vehicle across rough ground, a first halting step towards 'autonomous transit' and continuous motion.

With very high-speed integrated circuitry (VHSIC) it is hoped it will be possible to apply intelligent logic to dynamic, constantly changing environments, within reasonable limits of space and cost. In a manned aircraft, artificial intelligence could be applied to the sensor processing and cockpit display systems, co-ordinating the operation of navigation/attack and electronic warfare systems and providing some of the unique capabilities of a two-crew aircraft in a smaller, lighter and cheaper single-pilot aircraft.

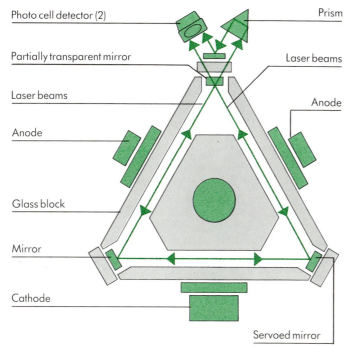

Photo cell detector (2)
Prism
Partially transparent mirror
Laser beams
Laser beams
Anode
Anode
Glass block
Mirror
Cathode
Servoed mirror

RING LASER GYRO

Lasers are not yet weapons themselves but they have applications across military technology especially in target designation and range finding. They have also been used to create a completely new kind of gyroscope — the ring laser gyro in which variations in movement of a platform can be interpreted as variations in frequency of laser beams arranged in an isoceles triangle. A computer interprets the signals into navigational data

Using voice-recognition equipment, the pilot could even talk to the robotic back-seater. But it is in unmanned systems that the potential of artificial intelligence is greatest. Genuinely 'smart' weapons (the term 'brilliant' is sometimes used for these) are only part of the story.

Unmanned vehicle systems (UVS) will be used to fill a few of the roles filled by the manned aircraft, but will also create a great many new missions particularly in hazardous or inhospitable environments, where the risk to the human operator is so great that the cost of the mission is largely determined by the cost of keeping the operator safe. This logic may apply to any number of situations. Airborne examples might include low-level reconnaissance, attacks on heavily defended airfields or ships, or chaff-bombing in front of an attacking force.

On land, robotics could create an unsleeping sentry with an infinite attention span, perfect night vision and no interest in military pay or benefits. Robotic vehicles could be sent on suicide missions behind enemy lines, and lie indefinitely in undetectable ambush — they will be far smaller than manned vehicles. Also, their small size would make the army more mobile. In the nearer term, robotics could provide an efficient autoloader for a future tank's gun.

The most inhospitable environment of all for humans is the total vacuum of space. With their living environment, atmosphere and re-entry system, human astronauts take 15 to 20 times their weight into space, and every system has to be 100 per cent reliable or 100 per cent backed-up. Even then, their manipulative abilities are restricted by space-suits and by their bodies' insistence that there is an 'up' and a 'down'.

However space is almost a paradise for robots, being clean, free of gravity (so that effort and power requirements are reduced) and replete with boundless supplies of energy. This is not to say that robots will oust people from space; the human ability to improvise has saved many missions, and will continue to do so. But the economic advantages of using robotic systems wherever possible, and of pushing the development of robotic space systems as fast as can be managed, are overwhelming.

Current programmes in which military funding is being poured into computer research are more than just another technical fad. They reflect the fact that computing can no longer be regarded simply as a tool for C^3I, aerospace engineering or naval architecture. Computing is a major military science in its own right — and it may be the most important of all of them.

2 AIR WARFARE

Air warfare has passed through many changes in its relatively short history, with major swings in emphasis taking place almost every decade. The cause, in many cases, has been developing technology. New systems and new concepts have tended to render the last generation's weapons and tactics ineffective before they have matured and the challenge to the designer is to anticipate the inevitable counter-development and, if possible, to outrun it. Neither does yesterday's threat disappear automatically as a new one emerges. The threat to airpower assets is cumulative. An excellent example is anti-aircraft artillery (AAA). A heavy concentration of light AAA, even if it is aimed by little more than dead reckoning, can be a serious threat to even the most advanced systems, just as it has been since the 1940s.

The development of military aircraft between now and the year 2000 will have to address a number of important changes in the threat. New micro-electronic techniques are already increasing the capability which can be built into mobile and affordable missile systems. The ability of missiles to threaten air bases is beginning to exceed the resources of defensive technology and all aspects of airpower now have to take account of the probability that airfields will be hit. Even the sceptics have to acknowledge that electronic warfare has become as dangerous as physical attack; militarily, the aircraft cut off from the outside world or deprived of its sensor information is as useless as if it had been repulsed by fire.

The combat aircraft will not be rendered obsolete. Its unparalleled mobility remains untouched, and it is mobility which makes it possible for a relatively small number of systems to be effectively used over a vast area. Current and future plans point the way to survival for future combat aircraft.

Before any all-new aircraft arrive in service, derivatives of existing types will meet developments in the threat. 'Mid-life update' programmes of this kind are essential to an economic defence policy, taking advantage of the enormous investment in the original development and production of the basic versions. One of the biggest of these programmes is the development of the F-15E Eagle long-range strike fighter.

The F-15E shows how much can be done with an existing design. The original F-15 is a pure fighter — 'not a pound for air-to-ground' was the watchword used during development. But the incorporation of new technology can transform the Eagle into a highly effective bomber.

The airframe of the F-15E reflects the fact that designers are appreciating the importance of integrating the external load with the airframe; it is useless to create a refined aerodynamic design and then weigh and drag it into mediocrity with bombs, multiple racks and fuel tanks. In the F-15E, the extra fuel needed for the strike mission is carried in specially designed 'conformal' tanks, blended into the fuselage sides. Long, shallow pylons under the new tanks carry the bomb load in tandem rows, so that the front bomb's slipstream blankets the bombs to its rear. It is estimated that the second bomb in a row creates half the drag of the first, and the third creates half the drag of the second.

The F-15 was one of the first fighters to carry a radar/missile system which could pick out a low-level target, against a background of ground clutter, track it and guide a weapon on to it. Such systems are now standard for any new first-line fighter, and present a major threat to strike aircraft. However, they are still at the edge of capability for a fighter radar, and the existence of the F-15E is evidence that the US Air Force still believes that they are not all-capable. The F-15E still relies on low altitude, and powerful built-in electronic jamming and deception equipment, for its survival.

The F-15E will also be able to take cover under weather or darkness, and still complete its mission. The key to this capability is the way in which the original Hughes APG-63 radar has been developed. Like other contemporary airborne radar systems, APG-63 is 'modular' in design. Its various components are designed to be removed individually for maintenance, inspection or replacement, and this also facilitates development. In the F-15E's APG-70 radar, a new-technology signal processor distils more information from the raw radar return, and provides terrain avoidance and unbelievably precise mapping data, almost to the point where the radar could be used to track moving vehicles on the ground. In the air-to-air mode, the new processor can even identify an airborne target by measuring the distinctive rhythm which the front face of the engine puts into the radar echo.

In the final attack phase, the F-15E will often be able to shut down its radar with its treacherous emissions. Instead, it will use infra-red 'thermal imager' sensors and an advanced head-up display to project a view of the outside world ahead of the pilot, making the aircraft essentially independent of daylight. A narrow-angle (or telephoto-type) thermal imager will allow the weapon system operator in the rear seat to inspect and classify targets at long range. Thermal imagers are, in some ways, superior to daylight for military purposes; heat signatures distinguish

Below: *Beyond current plans for derivative developments of existing designs such as the F-15 lies the USAF's requirement for 'Advanced Tactical Fighter' (ATF). This short runway capable proposal from McDonnell Douglas features vectoring nozzles and canard winglets*

Right: *The F-15 Eagle was originally designed as an air to air fighter but this view of an F-15D reveals the formidable load of ordnance the aircraft can lift. The derivative F-15E is being designed to carry its weapons load conformally*

instantly between active and knocked-out vehicles, or between real targets and decoys, and make targets more visible against a background of soil or vegetation.

Another advanced development of an existing type, with even more radically improved performance, is the General Dynamics F-16F, due to replace the current F-16C in production by the early 1990s. Development has taken a different course: while the avionics and sensors of the F-16F will be similar to those of the F-16C, the aerodynamics are completely new. It has a unique 'cranked-arrow' wing. This offers many of the advantages of the slender delta, an idealised supersonic configuration. It allows a long, slim airframe without excessive weight, much of the wing falls behind the primary shock-wave from the nose and it provides tremendous carrying space for weapons. But the plain delta has disadvantages too. Its pitch controls are close to the centre of gravity, and must therefore produce a strong downforce (trim drag) to balance the aircraft. Its span is short, so it is inefficient at low speeds or in a

turn, and its manoeuvrability is hampered further by the fact that the short trailing edge has to provide both pitch and roll control.

The cranked-arrow wing of the F-16F is, in a sense, two wings in one. The inner section is a highly swept, deep and capacious slender delta, while the outer section is a thin-section, sharp-lipped wing of moderate sweep. Trim drag is reduced by moving the centre of gravity aft of the centre of lift, taming the flying characteristics with the automatic flight control system. Not only is there a greater length of trailing edge available for pitch and roll control, but the leading-edge flaps on the outer wing are, uniquely, also used for augmented roll control. The F-16XL pitches and rolls faster than the basic F-16.

The F-16F also uses a concept called 'vortex lift'. At moderate to high angles of attack, the junctions between the wing and the fuselage, and between the inner and outer wings, generate high-energy, swirling vortices. As these stream back over the wing, they actually stabilise airflow, reduce pressures above the wing and increase the ratio of lift to

Left: *An F-16 was modified with canard winglets and a digital flight control system for the AFTI (Advanced Fighter Technology Integration) programme to explore 'decoupled control'*

Below: *The F-16XL with its cranked arrow wing, testbed for the F-16F*

drag. Currently, vortex lift is one of the black arts of aerodynamics being hard to predict or simulate, but this may prove to be one of the most rewarding areas of research for new aerodynamic simulation computers in the next few years.

Thanks to its deep, large-area wing, the internal fuel capacity of the F-16F is 82 per cent greater than that of the standard F-16. More significantly, perhaps, it is 94 per cent of the internal fuel load of the F-15C, which has exactly twice as much installed power to feed. Under the wing are troughs for semi-recessed AIM-120 air-to-air missiles (these are no novelty, having been invented for the F-4 in the mid-1950s, but will be standard on future combat aircraft) and simple attachments for bombs and missiles, carried in drag-reducing tandem rows.

The F-16F is also one of the first aircraft to depend for its feasibility on new 'composite' materials. Composite materials are so called because they are made up of two separate elements: very fine fibres, some of which are

only as thick as a single molecule, and a 'matrix' which is poured around the fibres and sets hard. The matrix holds the fibres together; the strength of the material comes from the fibres themselves. The key to the qualities of composites is that very fine, pure fibres can be stronger than a steel strand of the same thickness (everyone remembers the puzzling fact that a spider's web is stronger than steel) and far stronger than aluminium. Even very strong metals such as titanium and beryllium only just approach the ultimate tensile strength of a composite, and these are very expensive and difficult to work with — beryllium is light, strong and virtually indifferent to heat but is, unfortunately, highly toxic.

The best known of the new fibres is carbon. Filaments of carbon were first produced in the 1960s, and proved extremely strong and not unreasonably costly. Carbon-fibre composite (CFC) usually consists of carbon fibres embedded in an epoxy resin matrix, related to some advanced adhesives. (In the USA, CFC is known as 'graphite-epoxy' or simply 'graphite'.) CFC use has steadily expanded since its invention. The US Navy's latest fighter, the F-18 Hornet, has CFC wing skins (the wing spars are aluminium and titanium). In 1983, the US Marine Corps took delivery of its first AV-8B Harrier IIs, with wings made almost entirely of CFC; weight is so critical on the Stovl (short take-off/vertical landing) Harrier that the use of CFC is a vital part of the design.

One increasingly important attribute of composite material is that it can be made up with the fibres aligned in any direction or combination of directions. If the fibres are criss-crossed in an even, symmetrical pattern, the resulting CFC skin will have uniform bending characteristics, like a metal component. But if the fibres run predominantly in a given direction, the material will be stiffer in one direction than another. In the F-16F this technique, 'aero-elastic tailoring', is used to absorb the peculiar bending loads of the cranked-arrow wing.

Following close behind the F-16F are a group of new Western fighters: Israel's Lavi, Sweden's JAS 39, Britain's Experimental Aircraft Prototype, France's ACX and the last two types' intended development, the multinational European Fighter Aircraft (EFA). All of them are in the same mould, with swept or cranked wings and canard foreplanes. Apart from JAS, all have ventral air intakes, and all have F-16-type cockpits with reclined seats. All use composite primary structure, with aero-elastic tailoring to increase flutter resistance without commensurately increased weight.

Why such uniformity? One reason is that many of the F-16's features have proved extremely successful. Another is that present technology makes the canard layout very attractive. The basic advantage of a canard is that it always provides lift; the conventional tail, by contrast, pushes the aircraft down to lift the nose, forcing the wing to work harder to sustain level flight and adding a great deal of drag. A 'close-coupled' canard, just ahead of the wing, contributes a great deal of lift and makes it possible to reduce the size, weight and drag of the main wing. In a supersonic fighter, which usually needs a long forward fuselage because of wave-drag considerations, the use of a canard allows a truncated rear fuselage so saving an immense amount of weight. But the canard has a drawback which has, in the past, restricted its use: if it is used to develop a powerful pitching moment it makes the aircraft unstable. As the pitch angle increases so does the power of the canard, and the aircraft will pitch out of control. Early canard aircraft either used small foreplanes, like Rutan lightplanes, or conventional surfaces on the trailing edge of the wing for control (as in the XB-70 and the Viggen) and simply used the foreplane for trim.

Now, however, experience with pitch-unstable aircraft such as the SR-71 and F-16, together with advances in electronics, have made it possible to design aircraft which rely at all times on their automatic flight control systems (AFCS) for stability. Tiny control corrections, provided many times every second by the AFCS, make the unstable aircraft flyable and allow the designers to take full advantage of the canard layout.

Aircraft such as the new European fighter represent the next step beyond the F-16 generation, but the US Air Force is already planning a next-generation aircraft, the Advanced Tactical Fighter (ATF), of even higher performance. Due to enter service in the mid-1990s, ATF will combine long range with the ability to cruise and manoeuvre at supersonic speeds for sustained periods, at altitudes up to 70 000 feet.

To anyone familiar with the discussions of the late 1950s and early 1960s, when it was generally accepted that high Mach and high altitude was a recipe for certain destruction by SAMs (surface-to-air missiles), this feature of ATF will come as a surprise. But this was a case where the general view was wrong. As soon as 'high-fast' penetration was actually tried — in the course of 1963 — it was discovered that SAMs had certain inherent disadvantages, and that a 'high, fast sanctuary' still existed.

To reach its target the SAM has to accelerate

rapidly through the thick, low-altitude air, where wing area is a penalty. But to engage a manoeuvring target at high level, it needs wing area to provide manoeuvrability. The compromise is a difficult one, and usually means that the missile has only a limited ability to turn in the thin upper air. Most missiles are rocket-propelled and coast for most of their flight. In the case of such weapons, the ability to change direction at high level is strictly limited by the inertia available. Ramjet-powered weapons avoid this problem at the expense of others; it is difficult to make the engine operate efficiently over a wide range of speeds and altitudes, and the overall system tends to be more costly.

Also, most SAMs need guidance data from their launch units. Exceptions include infrared homing missiles, and large weapons which have their own active-radar guidance systems, but the former have a limited range, and the designer of the latter type is faced with a choice between a simple radar which is easy to detect and jam, and what would essentially be a fighter-type radar. But most missile systems include a ground-based radar in the guidance loop, to provide electronic counter-countermeasures (ECCM) characteristics at a reasonable cost. However this means that the system's response to target movement is not instantaneous. If the target turns, the ground-based system must detect the change in track for long enough to predict the new track. This must be converted into a control impulse, and transmitted to the missile; the missile's control surfaces then move, and only then does the missile start to change direction. The result is that there is a measurable lag in the system, not very large, but

enough to send the missile behind the target were it not for a certain amount of prediction built into the system: like a gun, the missile system aims ahead of the target. If the target is changing track in an unpredictable manner — and any turn is unpredictable — the missile will not hit it. With a heavy missile at high altitude, and an aircraft which can pull 2 to 2·5 g turns at supersonic speed, the missile designer is faced with a serious problem.

Aerodynamic design for supersonic cruise presents few problems; the engine is the main area which needs attention, and most of the technology for supersonic propulsion is already available. However, ATF could gain from the incorporation of new aerodynamic and structural technology. ATF configurations in published impressions have varied widely. Some resemble the F-16F — with the right engine and a variable inlet, the F-16F could probably sustain supersonic speed on dry thrust. Others use less blended configurations, with or without canards.

One radical candidate configuration is the forward-swept wing (FSW), being tested on the Grumman X-29A research aircraft. The FSW has some remarkable benefits. Swept wings have some undesirable characteristics; their tips stall first at high angles of attack, causing the aircraft to pitch upwards (because of the loss of lift aft) and simultaneously rendering the ailerons useless. Also, the effective aerodynamic sweep — measured at the quarter-chord — is less than the physical sweep of the structure, causing a certain weight penalty. The FSW turns these disadvantages inside out. An FSW stalls at the root and retains full lateral control until the wing is totally stalled. The aerodynamic sweep is

Anti-Air Missile Seeker

A long range air-to-air missile has to be comparatively large, both to accommodate enough propellant to sustain its flight and a target acquisition system powerful enough to pick up targets at appropriate ranges.
Miniaturisation of components has progressed far but having to use a gimballed radar antenna which locks onto a target, then generating automatic guidance commands, is still a critical factor. Designers striving to produce true 'fire and forget' weapons, whether surface-to-air (SAMs) or air-to-air (AAMs) have the further problem of building in resistance to electronic countermeasures without too great a penalty in size and cost

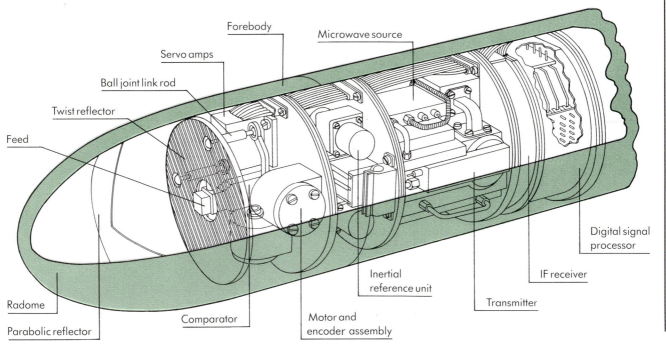

Forebody
Microwave source
Servo amps
Ball joint link rod
Twist reflector
Feed
Digital signal processor
Radome
Inertial reference unit
IF receiver
Parabolic reflector
Comparator
Motor and encoder assembly
Transmitter

greater than the structural sweep. Another benefit is that the FSW, with its thicker root aft of the aerodynamic centre, is inherently easy to integrate into a low-wave-drag, area-ruled design.

Until composites and aero-elastic tailoring were introduced, however, the FSW was impractical, because it is aero-elastically unstable. If the wing bends upwards at the tip, the upward air loads will increase and bend it further until it fails. Early high-subsonic FSW aircraft simply had heavy metal wing structures, but a supersonic metal FSW would have to be virtually solid. Composites change the picture. The upper and lower skins of the X-29 wing are specially tailored in the same direction. As the wing bends upwards the top skin, in compression, attempts to bend forwards. The lower skin, in tension, tries to bend aft. But the two are rigidly fastened together, so the 'shearing' forces in the tailored skins prevent the wing from bending.

The X-29 also has a thin-section supercritical wing with variable camber, designed for high lift combined with low supersonic drag. It has 'three-surface' longitudinal control, with a foreplane, manoeuvring flaps and trim flaps on the tail. The entire aircraft is designed for optimum lift distribution at supersonic speed, and at low speeds is highly unstable. While earlier aircraft have flown in unstable flight regimes with such systems, the X-29A is the first design in which a total AFCS failure might not leave a stable platform for pilot ejection.

Other advanced research programmes could contribute to ATF. Variable geometry of one kind or another will continue to be used for some specialised applications. Whether many new variable-sweep military aircraft will be in service in the year 2000 is questionable, simply because existing aircraft will still fill many of the requirements to which the technique is suited. A promising and potentially important technology, though, is smoothly variable camber. This has been an unattainable goal of aerospace for decades, and is finally being made possible for high-performance aircraft through the development of strong but flexible composite materials. Under the Mission Adaptive Wing (MAW) programme, a General Dynamics F-111 is being fitted with a thin-section wing, fitted with smoothly-faired leading-edge flaps and a continuously curved variable-camber trailing edge.

The MAW control surfaces provide roll control and increased lift at low speeds, like the conventional flaps and slats which they replace. The crucial difference is that they do not cause a massive drag rise when they are deflected. On the F-111 test-bed they will be operated automatically in several modes. They can be deflected downwards to

Two European contenders in the next generation agile fighter line up. They are the Swedish JAS 39 Gripen (right) and the French Dassault ACX (below). Both feature canard foreplanes and a primary structure made of composite materials

optimise the wing for higher lift in transonic manoeuvre; they can be programmed to seek the most efficient cruise setting at constant power and altitude; the outboard surfaces can deflect upwards in a hard manoeuvre, to reduce the peak load on the wing (this means that the wing can be more lightly built for the same flight load requirements); and the flaps can also move in response to gusts. An early-1980s McDonnell Douglas fighter design study shows where this could lead: it has a long-span, very-thin-section, unswept wing. Use of MAW techniques would make it possible to build a wing without a virtually solid structure.

Another important programme directly related to ATF will make use of an F-15, modified to operate from runways only a fraction as long as those needed by most current aircraft. Designed to use two-mile, hard-concrete runways, they suffer increasing performance penalties as the runway length available is reduced. The vulnerability of the runway is at last being appreciated; the countermeasure proposed by ATF planners is to provide for operations from damaged airfields. This will certainly mean operating from shorter field lengths. While it only takes a few hits to put an airfield's two-mile run-

ways out of action, it is much more difficult to eliminate every straight 1500-foot section, and it is much easier to repair an airfield to that level.

Five-hundred yards, or under one-sixth of the length of the standard NATO runway, is the field-length goal for the ATF. This is not quite as demanding as it sounds. Manoeuvrability requirements mean that two basics for short-take-off-and-landing (Stol) performance — low wing loading and high installed power — are already present on most modern fighters. To attain Stol performance, the USAF will fit the F-15 with canards and a vectoring and reversing engine nozzle.

While neither reversing nor vectoring is new, the combination of the two is innovative, as is the use which the US Air Force plans to make of it. The new nozzle will be able to reverse all or part of the engine's unreheated thrust, on the ground or in flight, and vector the full thrust of the engine some 30 degrees upwards or downwards. It will also be variable in area and internal profile to match speed and thrust, like the exhaust nozzles of current aircraft. Because a conventional circular nozzle incorporating all these features would be a mechanical nightmare, the new nozzle will be rectangular in cross-section with fixed sidewalls forming the short sides. Two sets of doors and cascades make up the long sides and, because they all move in the same plane, the nozzle is described as a 'two-dimensional' or '2-D' design.

The 2-D nozzle will be an integral part of the ATF and of its engine. It will be controlled by the engine's digital electronic engine control (Deec) which in turn will co-operate with the digital flight control system (DFCS). The nozzle will get its orders from the pilot either through the throttle lever and the Deec, or through the flight controls via the DFCS; as far as the pilot is concerned, the nozzle will be fully automatic.

The nozzle will operate at all times. The ATF will start its take-off roll with the throttle open, and the nozzle pointed aft, for maximum acceleration. At rotation speed — a good deal slower than that of current aircraft — the pilot will pull back on the stick, and the DFCS and Deec will deflect the nozzle upwards to force the nose up. Deflecting engine thrust upwards on take-off may seem odd, but a high-powered fighter has enough lift and power to get away with it.

In flight, the 2-D nozzle will provide added pitch control power for manoeuvring, particularly in what is called 'the upper left-hand corner'. This expression, derived from the shape of the standard performance chart, refers to flight at low airspeeds and high altitudes when aerodynamic controls are least effective. By very small adjustments of the nozzle angle, too, the 2-D system can provide zero-drag trim to balance the aircraft, and the in-flight reversing system provides rapid deceleration. The last-mentioned attribute could be a useful combat manoeuvre, because, unlike an airbrake, it gives a pursuer no visual 'cues' and could cause him to overshoot.

On landing, the 2-D nozzle's ability to reverse part or all of the exhaust, combined with movable cascades in the reverser ducts, will give the ATF pilot responsive, precise and decoupled control over forward speed. The vectoring facility could also be used as for pitch control, giving a canard ATF the advantages of a three-surface layout. Accurate control means accurate touchdowns, followed by a landing roll using full reverse thrust.

The 2-D nozzle is heavier than a conventional design. A nozzle, after all, is a pressure vessel and is most efficient when it is circular. However, it can reduce drag in cruising flight, saving fuel, it allows the use of a smaller, lighter tail or foreplane and eliminates the need for an airbrake.

The ATF's engines themselves are likely to mark a substantial step forward in basic gas-turbine technology; while producing about the same power as current large fighter engines, they will be hundreds of pounds lighter, much simpler and more ruggedly built. They will be very different in other ways, largely because the ATF is designed for sustained flight at supersonic speeds. The ATF engine will probably be more like a turbojet than a turbofan, with less than 20 per cent of the air bypassing the combustor; the amount of reheat boost required will set the exact figure, and the purpose of the bypass system will be to feed the afterburner with cool air and oxygen. Even without the augmentor in operation, the exhaust will be hot and pressurised enough to drive the aircraft at Mach 1·5 to 1·8.

The main design challenge will be heat, a factor of the aircraft's speed. At high Mach numbers, the pressure rise associated with ram recovery becomes extreme, and brings with it a high temperature rise. This is multiplied by the engine pressure ratio, and the result is that temperatures at the back of the engine, downstream of the compressor, rise very rapidly with increasing Mach number. Once they reach the maximum permissible levels, the only answer is to throttle the engine back. This cuts temperatures but simultaneously reduces the thrust and efficiency of the engine.

The use of sophisticated cooling techniques and new materials in the combustor, turbine and afterburner of future engines will not eliminate the problem, but will postpone its worst effects to higher Mach numbers. Future military engines may have combustors made of carbon-carbon materials, almost impervious to heat, if the problem of protecting them from oxidation can be overcome. Advanced blade aerodynamics will be used in the turbine discs, with the aim of getting equal or better efficiency out of fewer, thicker and shorter blades which can be more easily plumbed with complex internal cooling passages.

The new engine for ATF — based on the Pratt & Whitney PW5000, or General Electric GE37, both being developed under the Joint Advanced Fighter Engine (JAFE) programme — will benefit from new design techniques. Particularly, the design of the individual blade aerofoils has advanced, so that each short, thick, contoured blade, and each stage of the engine, will be able to compress the incoming air to a much greater degree than is possible with current technology components. The result is that the newer engines will attain higher pressure ratios, increasing both efficiency and power-to-weight ratio, with fewer stages. The cut in the number of stages means that the engine is lighter,

The Lockheed SR-71 Blackbird strategic reconnaissance aircraft has been setting the pace in very high speed, high altitude flight for over two decades. In its blended wing/body form, it showed some early aspects of 'stealth' technology

shorter and stiffer; the last-named quality is important, because a stiff engine can be designed to tighter tolerances, improving efficiency. Each stage, too, will have fewer blades, so the PW5000 and GE37 will have less than half as many blades as the comparably-sized F100 and F110 of today.

Improved technology in the basic design actually reduces some of the stresses on materials. If less energy is wasted through leakage between the stages of the engine, for example, the turbine needs to do less work and can be run at a lower temperature. The new blade sections tend to be thicker, reducing tensile stresses and making it easier to design efficient cooling systems. All these features will help make engines more reliable and more durable.

Digital electronic engine control (Deec) will be standard by the year 2000, and today's hydromechanical systems with their myriad pipes and valves will look as quaint as adding machines do now. The maturity of Deec technology will affect engine design in much the same way as mature fly-by-wire has affected airframe design: engineers will be able to design engines much closer to stall limits, with fewer allowances and margins and correspondingly better efficiency, with full confidence that the Deec can handle the situation. Where the two situations are different is that the Deec is not just an extra item of equip-

ment, it replaces something that is heavier, less reliable and costs more to build and maintain.

Complex 'variable-cycle' engines, which can change from turbofans to turbojets with the aid of internal valves, are probably not on the cards for ATF. A simpler system, the variable area bypass injector (VABI) might bring an overall benefit, however. It consists of a variable-area nozzle, similar to today's exhaust nozzle, installed between the turbine and augmentor so that it can expand the exit throat of the core at the expense of the bypass duct or vice versa. By slight changes in bypass ratio, it is claimed, the VABI can improve transonic and supersonic thrust and reduce subsonic fuel consumption.

All the new features will be integrated through the aircraft's avionics systems, with the Deec, the fire-control system, and the AFCS constantly exchanging data and controlling the variable nozzle, engine and flight controls to give the best possible response to the pilot's control inputs. As well as allowing 'carefree manoeuvring' over an enormous flight envelope, recent tests have shown how remarkable accuracies can be achieved by 'dumb' ordnance, such as free-fall bombs and cannon shells, when the fire-control system is closely coupled to an advanced AFCS. Possibly, such integration will lead to new 'uncoupled' manoeuvres — either changing

attitude without changing flightpath, or changing flightpath without changing attitude — for air combat or weapons delivery. Early tests with such techniques, however, have shown that they may be less useful in practice than computer simulations had suggested.

ATF represents the mainstream of combat aircraft development, the basic dual-mission fighter/attack aircraft. It will serve alongside some more specialised types, some of them evolved from designs which are already in service.

Perhaps the most fascinating of current combat aircraft, if only because of the impenetrable blanket of secrecy which has covered its entire development, is the Lockheed F-19, better known as the Stealth fighter. Techniques and concepts relating to Stealth have been applied in the design of the Eurofighter and the F-16F, and will be a part of any ATF configuration, but these are still a far cry from aircraft such as the F-19 and the Northrop Advanced Technology Bomber, which rely on Stealth as their primary means of survival.

Stealth is not a single technical breakthrough. Rather, it is a matter of letting the electronic warfare team design the airframe. The definition of a Stealth aircraft starts with an analysis of the sensors which an enemy will use to detect it, track it and guide a weapon to it. These include radar of different wavelengths, thermal systems and electro-optical devices in the visual spectrum. The aircraft is then configured and constructed to offer the smallest possible signature in each spectrum.

Fundamentals of Stealth design include the elimination of vertical planes and sharp right angles from the configuration, which assumes a fluid, blended shape. The engines must be concealed behind long inlet and exhaust tunnels. Composites are preferable to metals for the primary structure. The object is to reduce the radar image as far as possible before resorting to the use of radar-absorbent material (RAM) which tends to add weight. RAM, however, is used on the edges of the airframe, and in the inlet ducts.

Attaining high levels of Stealth presents operational problems. Sustained supersonic speed is probably ruled out because of aerodynamic heating; external stores are taboo, a major problem on any fighter-type aircraft; so is the use of active radar, even for terrain-following or navigation.

However, the benefits of Stealth are potentially vast. Opposing missile systems may be rendered useless; by the time the Stealthy attacker is detected, it may well be within the minimum range of the missile. Increasing the power of the radar, however, makes the missile system easier to detect and to avoid, and makes it a more prominent target for anti-radar missiles. The reduction in radar cross-section may well be enough, in real-world

Left: *The McDonnell Douglas AV-8B is a descendant of the original British P.1127 VTOL technology demonstrator of the early 1960s. Meanwhile the unfulfilled challenge in Stovl technology is a short take-off, vertical landing combat aircraft capable of supersonic flight. 'Plenum chamber burning' is being developed using a BAe Harrier's Pegasus turbofan as the basis, the PCB providing the increased thrust for supersonic flight. This test rig (**right**) is used to explore the problems of re-ingesting hot gas exhaust during the hover*

*Military aircraft are becoming increasingly important as sensor platforms. USAF Lockheed TR-1s (based on the original U2 high altitude reconnaissance aircraft) carry sensor systems in their wing pods capable of detecting emissions from hostile ground transmitters at ranges of several hundred kilometres (**left**).The Boeing E-3A AWACS with its prominent rotodome (**above**) is perhaps the best known of the growing number of airborne early warning and control aircraft.*

conditions, to prevent a fighter's look-down, shoot-down radar-missile system from working. Apparently, highly secret trials of F-19 and other prototypes have been successful enough to prompt major production.

A different type of specialised military aircraft is the advanced short take-off/vertical landing (Astovl) fighter. Military planners are now looking again at the range of threats facing airfields, and wondering whether ATF's 500-yard field length might be a lot to expect after a withering shower of submunitions.

The Astovl has yet to find a place in firm military development plans. Stovl aircraft tend to be more expensive than conventional aircraft of the same flight performance, and the argument for adding performance or numbers in the air with the help of a little cheap concrete on the ground is persuasive. But interest in Stovl is bound to increase. Counter-airfield weapons continue to be improved, to the point where they can disable a well-defended airfield with protected hangars and ground facilities. The short-field capability planned for ATF is a tremendous step forwards, but the Astovl offers further advantages. While Harriers generally need a similar take-off distance to that proposed for ATF — about 1200 feet — they have a much lower take-off speed, which helps operations from uneven surfaces. Meanwhile, many of the features which conventional wisdom has cited as disadvantages of the Stovl type have been specified for the ATF. The added complexity of vectored thrust is one example.

Literally dozens of Stovl concepts have been proposed, and not a few of them have been tested in flight. They have ranged in complexity from the tail-sitter or VATOL (vertical attitude take-off and landing), which needs no extra mechanical systems for lift and just a simple low-speed control system, to a six-engined fighter with four engines in swivelling pods on the wingtips and two more installed vertically in the fuselage. Most have failed, more or less abysmally, and apart from the British-developed Harrier only the mediocre Soviet Yak-36 has seen service.

The success of the Harrier makes its layout very attractive as a basis for the Astovl. The fundamental change between the Harrier and the new aircraft is the addition of afterburners to the front nozzles, a technique called plenum-chamber burning (PCB). Like conventional reheat, PCB provides the thrust/weight ratio needed for supersonic flight and transonic manoeuvre, but it provides extra thrust at the front of the engine so that the thrust can still pass through the centre of gravity and the aircraft can hover.

PCB presents a number of technical challenges. One of the most basic problems is maintaining a stable and efficient burn in a very cool, low-velocity airstream. Another problem area is common to many high-speed Stovl aircraft. Like any aircraft with reheat, they produce a huge volume of hot exhaust air. Conventional aircraft simply leave it behind, but a hovering jet could re-ingest the hot air into its engine intakes, causing the engine to overheat very quickly. Current development work is aimed at quantifying some of these potential problems.

Other technologies are also under study for the Astovl. One quite promising system, based on the use of ejectors or jet-pumps, has been developed by de Havilland Canada. An ejector is an open-ended duct into which a high-pressure, high-speed airstream is injected through a nozzle half-way along its length. A combination of friction, mixing effects and pressure differentials draws outside air into the duct, and creates a high-mass, low-velocity airstream which is very efficient at low airspeeds — as are encountered in the case of a hovering Stovl aircraft. The improved propulsive efficiency means that the ejector can boost the thrust available from a jet engine by as much as 70 per cent. Also, it promises a great deal of thrust from a cool airstream, reducing the recirculation problem. The system forms the basis of a General Dynamics design know as the E-7, which may be tested in the form of a large-scale wind-tunnel model in 1988.

Another new concept, at an earlier stage of development, is the 'tandem fan', which is considered very promising by Rolls-Royce. The starting point for the tandem fan is a conventional augmented turbofan engine, but the first two stages of the fan are separated from the last stage and the core engine by a long driveshaft and straight duct. This transfer section incorporates an arrangement of cascades, auxiliary inlets and blockers which can separate the engine airflow into two streams. Air entering the main inlet passes through the front fan stages and exhausts vertically through a separate outlet, directly behind the fan. The rear fan stage and core breathe through auxiliary inlets and exhaust at the rear, through an augmented nozzle. Rolls-Royce has designed a version of this system, called a hybrid fan, in which the front stream exhausts through vectorable nozzles.

Advanced supersonic Stovl aircraft will bring the benefits of Stovl to a wider variety of missions. By the year 2000 they could be replacing types like the F-16 and Harrier II for offensive support, moving quickly to suppress threatening artillery or missile systems, engaging enemy support aircraft and hitting armour with multiple-warhead munitions. They will operate with relative immunity from counter-air operations; advanced electronic systems, with their capacity for self-test and self-diagnosis and their ability to function after partial failures, will make the Stovl fighter reliable and rugged for off-base operation. The sort of technology that is applied to the ATF in search of ultimate performance against high-value targets will be adapted to another end in the Stovl fighter, to give it quick reaction and high reliability. It will be a tough, independent, 'kick the starter and jump aboard' fighting machine.

Undoubtedly the supersonic Stovl will be developed in parallel for naval operations. The Harrier has already demonstrated that a Stovl aircraft designed purely for land-based operation needs no modification to operate from a ship. As the development of the Sea Harrier shows, however, the shipboard version of a future Stovl will have rather different equipment and weapons, suited to its likely targets; it will have a powerful radar, and developed, long-range versions of missiles such as the AIM-120 or the anti-ship Sea Eagle. It might well carry longer-range weapons such as Stealth cruise missiles.

Given the armoury of advanced weapons that it will need, and the sophistication of its systems, the naval Stovl will not be found on the helideck of the average frigate. Neither will it be routinely operated off a converted merchant ship. Tailored Stovl carriers will be real warships, well protected and well defended and with plenty of capacity for weapons; it will not make sense to put the Stovl fighter on anything less.

Stovls will find a place aboard conventional supercarriers as well, for a number of good reasons. They can be launched regardless of relative wind and without taking up time on the catapult. Similarly, they can be recovered without blocking the landing deck. Thanks to their ability to 'stop, and then land', as Stovl aviators put it, they can also operate in conditions which would halt normal carrier operations. In the Falklands, Harriers were recovered safely when forward visibility was less than the length of the carrier.

While the naval Stovl fighter will have a specially built carrier as its regular base, there will certainly be merchant-ship-based auxiliary carriers, possibly operating a mix of navy and air force aircraft. Fitted with prefabricated hangars and decks, and carrying containerised control and defence systems, these ships will support amphibious operations and long-distance deployments. For most countries, navy fighter forces will become the permanent core of their rapid-deployment air power, augmented by air force squadrons in time of need.

Alongside the Stovl fighter will be Stovl support aircraft. In all probability, a single medium-sized subsonic aircraft will be developed to serve in a number of different roles: airborne warning and control, probably with new electronically scanned 'conformal' antennae in the wing leading edges and fuselage sides, rather than a rotodome; transport and support; long-range strike and defence, acting simply as a platform for sensors and cruise missiles; anti-submarine warfare; and electronic intelligence-gathering. Many of the different versions would be equipped to serve as tankers. Different types of high-bypass, tandem-fan layouts could provide the power for such aircraft.

Generally, over land as well as over water, the number and importance of aircraft which are primarily sensor platforms is increasing. So far, though, the aerospace world has tended not to look at these types as a homogenous group but that is what they are. All of them — from the exotic SR-71, through converted second-hand 707s, down to modified King Airs — are elements of the C^3I

(command, communications, control and intelligence) or the 'military information' world.

An active rumour in the USA has it that the SR-71 is to be replaced within a few years by a new penetrating reconnaissance aircraft, capable of 3500 to 4000-mile an hour speeds at altitudes above 120 000 feet. Such a vehicle would pose extreme problems, even for the most advanced SAM systems. Its development would be entirely feasible; power would probably be provided by supersonic-combustion ramjets, fuelled with liquid hydrogen which would additionally serve to cool the airframe. Lifting-body configurations with adequate stability at Mach 6 have been successfully tunnel-tested, and offer adequate volume for the low-density fuel. The main problem would be emulating the SR-71's greatest asset — its global mobility — given that in-flight refuelling with liquid hydrogen is probably impossible.

Another important C³I asset is the U-2/TR-1 high-altitude surveillance platform. The aircraft exists, its development is paid for, and despite its age it is very difficult to improve on its altitude, payload and endurance. It is also designed so that new 'payloads' — surveillance or communications equipment — can be built into removable pallets and pods and simply installed in the aircraft.

High-capacity communications links and long-range surveillance systems will create a need for communications and surveillance aircraft, the airborne watchtowers of the 'extended battlefield'. There is an active controversy in this area, typified in the current US programme to develop a long-range, high-resolution radar system to pinpoint tank formations behind enemy lines. Some believed that the system would be more effective and more versatile if the radar and its operators were carried aboard a Boeing 707; others contend that such a system represents too easy and too valuable a target for MiG-31 long-range fighters, and would rather put the operators in earthbound shelters and the electronics in a stealthy TR-1 at 75 000 feet. The 707 advocates seem to be carrying the day.

Other C³I aircraft include the US Navy's Boeing E-6A, another 707 development, equipped to communicate with ballistic missile submarines; the US Air Force's E-4B, which provides the same service for land-based missiles; and airborne warning and control types such as the Boeing E-3 Sentry and the Soviet Ilyushin 'Mainstay-A'. Again, there is concern over the vulnerability of the E-3 to fighter attacks; this is probably of less concern to the Soviet Air Force, because the 'Mainstay' is thought to be primarily intended for continental defence.

Also in the C³I field. are the many and proliferating systems designed to intercept or degrade the enemy's C³I systems. These include such aircraft as the US Army's RU-21 Guardrail, which is designed to monitor tactical communications; the US Navy's EP-3E, designed to locate and classify Soviet battle groups by their passive emissions, using a highly sophisticated onboard computer; and the Soviet Union's Il-20 'Coot-A' jamming platform. All in all, the number of aircraft involved is considerable (see Chapter 8).

Another air mission of great importance is airlift. The realisation, in recent years, that conflict may be short and intensive, that small and relatively cheap weapons pose a threat to the largest ships, and that effective airlift could be a decisive factor may have concentrated some minds on the subject.

The sole representative of the state-of-the-art airlifter is the McDonnell Douglas C-17, due to enter service in the early 1990s. The C-17 is an entirely conventional aircraft, with a metal primary structure and off-the-shelf, commercial-type engines. The main innovation in its design is its complex and very rigid flap system, which extends into the path of the engine exhaust. The exhaust itself is deflected and also drags outside air over the flap. The system makes it possible for the C-17 to fly very slowly at high weights, and to operate from 3000-foot runways. Also of note, and presenting a great engineering challenge, are the C-17's thrust reversers, which are designed to give the big freighter the ground handling of a London taxi without creating chaos on a crowded ramp.

The C-17 is a remarkable aircraft in many ways. Its overall dimensions are close to those of the older C-141, but its payload capacity is closer to that of the giant C-5, and its ability to accept outsize loads is virtually the same. Meanwhile, its Stol performance betters the C-130, and the practical aspects of combat airlift missions, such as the ability to operate at high rates from a single runway with a limited apron space, have been addressed as never before.

There are, however, still a number of active controversies in airlift, and they are reflected in many current designs. One of them is the ability to operate from quickly prepared strips. But how quickly should the airstrip be prepared? The amount of effort needed to accommodate and service different types of aircraft varies enormously. Army manpower is measured in battalion/days; a base for a Stol aircraft such as a de Havilland Buffalo can be prepared in 0·5 battalion/day, a C-130 base takes more than six times as much effort and a base for heavy airlifters

The Lockheed C-130 Hercules is the world's most widely used combat airlifter, serving with many air forces. In the USAF at least it is due to be supplemented by the technically ambitious C-17 which will have all the C-130's short field performance plus much greater range and heavy lift capability

such as C-5s and C-141s takes 60 battalion/ days to build. The length of runway is not the only factor concerned; 'flotation', or the load imposed on the runways and taxiways, is also important. Good flotation is desirable, but costly, demanding a heavy and bulky landing gear. The C-17 specification called for less flotation than the C-5 requirement; instead, its ground manoeuvrability is supposed to allow it to operate within confined areas of paved runway. The Soviet Il-76 was obviously designed to allow repeated operations on dirt strips, and has a massive, 20-wheel landing gear with fat low-pressure tyres.

Combat survivability is another issue. While the Soviet Union has routinely fitted tail guns to its freighters, the West has tended to assume that its transports will never come under fire. This attitude seems to be changing. The C-17 may well carry chaff/flare dispensers, and an electronic warfare suite for airlifters is under intensive research study.

A future tactical transport, developed to replace the Lockheed C-130, would reflect survivability considerations to an even greater degree. Use of a technique such as upper-surface-blowing (USB), as demonstrated on NASA's Quiet, Short-Haul Research Aircraft, could be important. USB not only provides excellent Stol performance, but also confers remarkable lift and agility at climb-out speeds, and provides natural engine shielding against heat-seeking weapons.

A large aircraft also provides considerable scope for built-in protection: self-sealing fuel tanks, widely separated fuel and hydraulic lines, extensive Kevlar protection around vital areas, and son on. With multiple control surfaces and an 'adaptive' automatic flight control system, a combat airlifter would be able to survive and even complete its mission after suffering airframe damage.

*Air-to-air missiles come in several varieties, configured for specific missions. The AIM-7 Sparrow (**left**) teamed with the F-15 Eagle uses semi-active homing for guidance. The Eagle's big, multi-mode radar provides constant illumination of the target and thus reflected emissions on which the Sparrow's much smaller radar seeker can home. Heat seeking missiles such as the French R550 Matra Magic here seen wing tip mounted on a French Air Force Mirage F.1 (**below left**) have much shorter range but are 'fire-and-forget' weapons in that the target's own heat emissions from jet efflux or friction heated airframe provide the emissions on which the missile can home. The Magic can operate at ranges from below 0·5 to 6 km*

Aircraft Armament

High speed on the ATF; virtual invisibility for the F-19; passive protection for the airlifter: all point to the tremendous threats facing modern airpower, many of them posed by new types of missile.

It took 20 years from the start of guided missile development to the first conflict in which they played a major role, the air battles over Viet Nam. Even then, many air-to-air engagements came down to gunfire, and the simplest air-to-air missiles (AAMs) were the only ones which worked with any consistency. Surface-to-air missiles (SAMs) were successful, largely as a result of being fired in immense numbers, but their main function was to force the attackers to use lower altitudes, within anti-aircraft artillery (AAA) envelopes.

The Arab-Israeli war of 1973 saw the SAM and the anti-tank missile used effectively for the first time, but it was not until 1982, in Lebanon and the Falklands, that AAMs and air-to-surface missiles truly functioned as advertised. Anti-ship missiles managed to hit ships, wide-aspect AAMs were effective in off-the-tail attacks, and snap-up radar-guided AAMs brought down two MiG-25s.

The Exocet's airframe, motor and warhead are quite conventional. Only an expert could tell Sidewinder and Sparrow AAMs used in 1982 from those used between 1965 and 1972. The key change has been electronics. Smarter processing of the raw data has made the weapons far more able to discriminate between target and not-target. Essentially, with a few exceptions, that is the main trend in missile design.

Regardless of the launch platform or the

intended class of target, missile development is driven by a number of factors. One of the most important is to achieve reliability in the real world; designers and programme managers have become more cautious and conservative since the 1960s. Another is the development of the target, which may become inherently more difficult to kill, as with the development of new armour for tanks, or embody new countermeasures, such as reduced radar cross-section on an aircraft.

Once these basic requirements are met, a third consideration comes into play: survival of the launch platform. In the case of the aircraft, the first step is to reduce the time taken to track the target, launch the missile and guide it to impact. If possible, the weapon should be a 'fire-and-forget' type which receives no commands after launch, but fire-and-forget is not the ultimate protection for the launch aircraft. It would be even better if the missile could be fired into the general area of its target, and hit it without requiring exact designation by the launch aircraft.

Missiles for different targets and different launch envelopes are all moving along the road to greater autonomy, and have reached different stages. Short-range AAMs have proven their fire-and-forget capability in combat, over a wide launch envelope. The AIM-9L Sidewinder has, in the process, become a legend in its own time. Capable of homing in on the heat generated by skin friction, it can be launched almost head-on to the target with very high reliability.

Current medium-range missiles still require the help of the launch fighter's radar to illumi-

Right: The Hughes AN/APG-63 multi mode radar can operate in an air-to-ground navigation and attack mode or air-to-air, acquiring targets and illuminating them for missile attack. The system and its computer software has been kept constantly updated but its complexity reveals the maintenance and readiness problems faced by high technology armed forces

nate the target, all the way to detonation. The main improvement in the 1970s, apart from look-down, shoot-down performance, has been track-while-scan. As the phrase suggests, this means that the launch fighter can provide illumination for the missile while still scanning and monitoring other targets. The system does not go blind to other targets throughout the missile's flight time.

The new Hughes AIM-120 Amraam (advanced medium-range AAM) is expected to change this situation. It embodies a miniature inertial guidance system and a complete radar system. Under some circumstances it can be launched on a pre-programmed track towards the target and will home on to it using its own radar. Alternatively, it can receive new guidance data in flight.

A future version of Amraam is expected to feature some type of air-breathing engine, giving it greater range and longer-lasting power. The latter attribute is important, because it enables the missile to perform sustained manoeuvres towards the end of its flight. However, development of the current Amraam is taking longer than expected and any future version is some time from entering service.

Fire-and-forget capability is spreading through the world of tactical air-to-surface missiles (ASMs). Anti-ship weapons such as Exocet, or the newer and more advanced British Aerospace (BAe) Sea Eagle, require no assistance after launch, due to the slow speed and large size of the target and the relative ease of picking out a ship against sea clutter. The first effective fire-and-forget overland ASMs were anti-radiation missiles (ARMs); the latest generation of ARMs, represented by the BAe Alarm and Texas Instruments Harm, are faster, can seek targets over a wider spread of wavelengths and are much more capable of dealing with countermeasures. Alarm embodies a particularly interesting feature: in one operating mode it can be boosted to altitude, cut its motor and descend slowly by parachute, presenting a sustained threat to any radar below. ARMs are the only missiles which can work by intimidation: the target radar may escape destruction by shutting itself down, but at the cost of letting the attacking aircraft through. Another advantage of the new weapons is their small size, making it practicable to carry them for self-defence.

The Hughes Maverick was the first fire-and-forget ASM for use against precision, non-emitting targets. It is now being followed into production by the much improved infrared (IR) version; as in the case of other thermal systems, the IR spectrum provides significant improvements in daylight capability, as

A Tornado GR 1 interdictor/strike aircraft of the RAF equipped with the two large pods which contain the JP 233 airfield attack weapon system. The pods contain two kinds of submunition, direct penetrators to pierce concrete runways and delayed action mines to hold up repair attempts

well as operating by night with no reduction in performance.

True fire-and-forget guidance, though, is still difficult to achieve economically on smaller weapons. Imaging IR of the quality needed to hit ground targets requires much better optical and electronic performance than anti-aircraft systems. IR homing is the goal for the long-range member of the European Trigat (third generation anti-tank) missile family, but this will not be operational until the mid-1990s.

A promising alternative to IR in some applications is millimetre-wave (MMW) radar. Advanced electronic techniques, MMW advocates believe, could make it possible to build a complete active radar seeker, including an

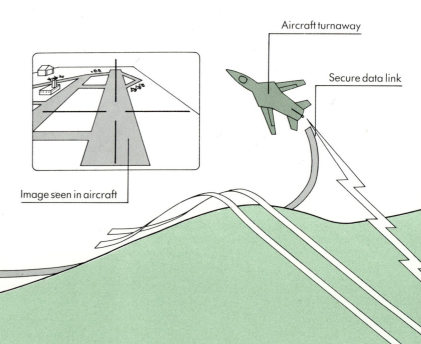

Aircraft turnaway

Secure data link

Image seen in aircraft

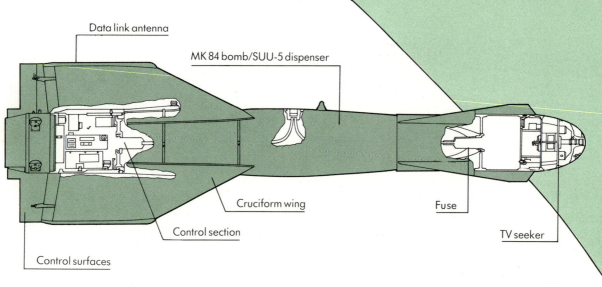

Data link antenna

MK 84 bomb/SUU-5 dispenser

Control surfaces

Control section

Cruciform wing

Fuse

TV seeker

AIRFIELD ATTACK

Counter-air warfare demands operations against airfields deep within hostile territory bristling with air defence, hence the importance of 'stand-off' precision-guided weapons. The USAF's GBU-15 unpowered glide bomb is an example, its cruciform wings allowing it to glide to its target while under positive control via secure data link from the launch aircraft (or a second aircraft), a tv in the weapon's nose sending back images of the target

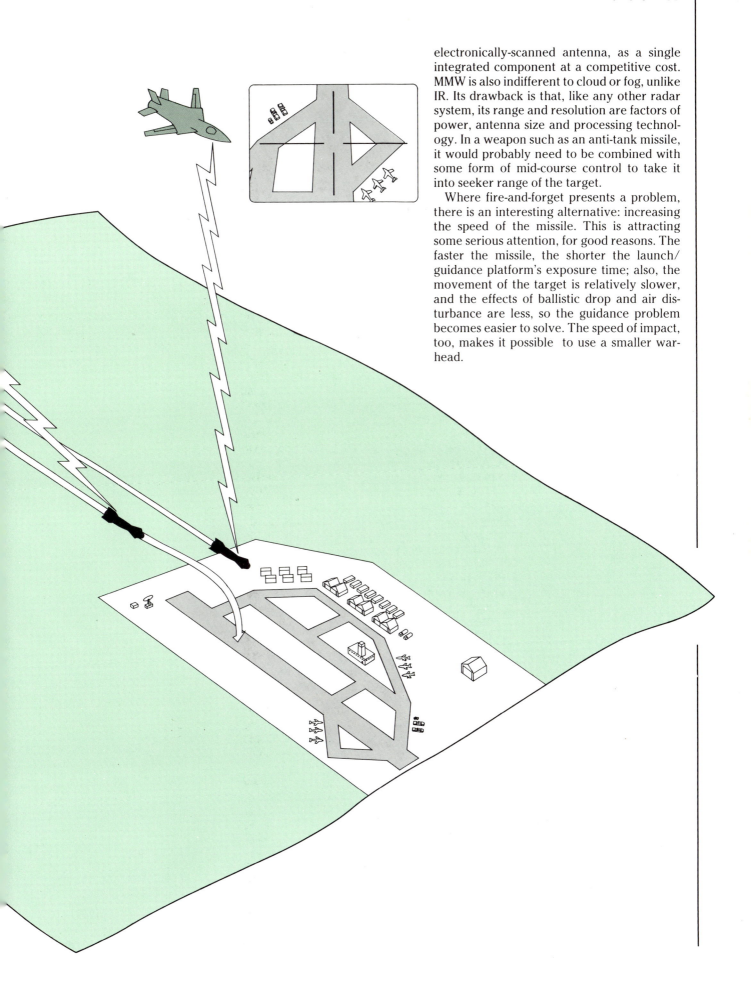

electronically-scanned antenna, as a single integrated component at a competitive cost. MMW is also indifferent to cloud or fog, unlike IR. Its drawback is that, like any other radar system, its range and resolution are factors of power, antenna size and processing technology. In a weapon such as an anti-tank missile, it would probably need to be combined with some form of mid-course control to take it into seeker range of the target.

Where fire-and-forget presents a problem, there is an interesting alternative: increasing the speed of the missile. This is attracting some serious attention, for good reasons. The faster the missile, the shorter the launch/guidance platform's exposure time; also, the movement of the target is relatively slower, and the effects of ballistic drop and air disturbance are less, so the guidance problem becomes easier to solve. The speed of impact, too, makes it possible to use a smaller warhead.

This weapon is called the hyper-velocity missile (HVM). It is mostly made up from a large, high-energy solid rocket motor, and is extremely fast, in the region of Mach 4·5. An HVM proposed by Vought needs no explosive warhead to destroy a tank: with an impact speed of nearly a mile per second, an assembly of metal rods will suffice. Flying almost a straight line to the target, the missile needs only a simple guidance system. For a flight time measured in seconds, the only control system required is a pair of control ports fed with hot gas by small, electronically-detonated explosive squibs. The result is that the missile is very small for its range and lethality, 20 rounds can be housed in a single pod, and a tactical fighter can carry several pods. It is potentially far cheaper than a precision-guided, fire-and-forget, anti-tank missile.

The HVM is guided by a laser radar system, somewhat simpler than a laser beam-riding device and capable of guiding multiple mis-

*The Hughes Maverick ASM is a powered air-to-surface missile with either a tv camera, laser seeker or imaging infra-red (IIR) seeker in the nose. This sequence (**left**) shows how an IIR Maverick generates images on the launch aircraft's cockpit display. The West German MW 1 in contrast (**above**) is an anti-armour, anti-airfield area weapon designed to strew submunitions widely. The JP 233 anti-airfield weapon has parachute retarded three-stage bomblets designed to do the damage (**right**) by first penetrating, then detonating thus heaving the concrete upwards*

siles. Sheer speed makes it possible to achieve multiple kills per pass, and like other optical beam-riders it is very difficult to jam.

Another alternative to the now traditional precision-guided ASM is based on combining modules to create a family of weapons based on common components. An example of trends in modern tactical air-to-surface weapons is the Northrop NV-150, proposed to the US Air Force in 1983. Designed for use against 'second echelon' armoured forces, the NV-150 has a plastic, reduced-observables airframe, a simple turbofan engine and a laser-gyro inertial navigation system, updated by navigational-satellite data, which contains no moving parts. All the main components are designed for low cost.

The NV-150 is a carrier vehicle for multiple small weapons known collectively as 'submunitions'. Underlying this change is the power of modern technology, non-nuclear

Right: *The US/Swiss developed ADATS missile system is a prototype laser beam riding weapon capable of both anti-tank and ground based air-defence applications*

Far Right: *The Vought hypervelocity missile capable of speeds up to Mach 4·5. Its destructive effects would be by kinetic energy alone — but nonetheless deadly to any armoured vehicle or aircraft it struck*

warheads. The use of chemical explosives has now reached the point where the only surface targets which merit the use of a heavy single warhead are ships and fortifications. Take, for example, the SG357 anti-runway munition developed as part of the British JP233 airfield-attack weapon. About the size of a waste-paper basket, the SG357 contains three charges which detonate in sequence. The first is a hollow charge which punches a hole in the runway. The second charge thrusts the weapon into the hole, where the third charge explodes; the trapped explosion breaks the concrete and heaves it upwards. The damage is far harder to repair than the crater caused by the heaviest conventional bomb, because the massive broken slabs must be lifted before the crater can be filled.

Submunitions can be delivered by a variety of vehicles which is a tremendous economic advantage. A single type of submunition can be produced for a variety of missiles, short-range and long-range, air-launched or surface-launched, increasing the production run and reducing costs. By the same token, a single basic type of missile, armed with different submunitions, can be used against a range of targets. Delivery systems can vary widely. In some British and German concepts sub-

munitions are ejected from a container attached to the aircraft. This has the advantage of delivering an extremely heavy load, but exposes the launch aircraft to defensive weapons. For the Advanced Tactical Fighter (ATF), the US Air Force has studied a gliding dispenser using lifting-body aerodynamics, and designed to blend with the carrier's aerodynamic configuration. This 'superconformal' weapon would reduce both drag and radar cross-section, and even without power it would have a stand-off range measured in miles.

Unguided submunitions have been developed for use against area targets such as airfields and surface-to-air missile sites; the next stage is the development of precision-guided submunitions (PGSMs) for use against small, mobile, protected targets such as tanks. One of the most extraordinary weapons in this category is the Avco Skeet. A small, saucepan-shaped object with a short wing in place of the handle, the Skeet is spun into the air and flies a wobbly path over a tank formation, its infra-red detector scanning the ground as the vehicle oscillates. When the detector signals the presence of a tank, the Skeet detonates above it, an explosive charge instantly forges the weapon's heavy metal base into a hypersonic

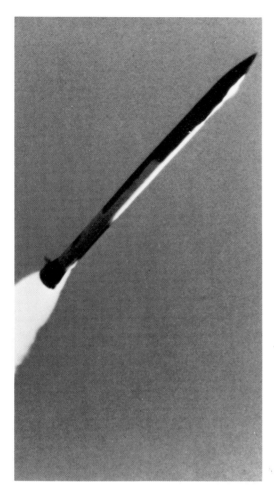

slug which hits the tank with enough force to pierce its top armour and destroy it. Skeets can be scattered from an airborne dispenser, but the alternative launcher is even more remarkable. A device resembling a small interplanetary lander is dispensed from a container and descends by parachute. Acoustic sensors detect the approach of a vehicle, measure its range and bearing and determine whether it is a tank. If a tank comes within range, the launcher will swivel and fire one of its three Skeets at it.

Weapons such as Skeet make it possible to combine the 'shotgun effect' with precision guidance, and hit groups of small targets at relatively long range. Such weapons will be supported in service by aircraft-borne systems such as Joint Stars (stand-off target acquisition radar system), which is being developed to provide accurate, real-time targeting data for USAF and US Army stand-off missiles.

Modular concepts will extend to guidance systems. The Rockwell AGM-130, a rocket-boosted version of the GBU-15 gliding bomb, will have interchangeable laser homing or tv-tracking heads. Alternatively, future air-to-surface stand-off weapons might standardise on a mass-produced, low-cost laser inertial

platform, which would be accurate enough to deliver submunitions within lethal distance.

With such advanced ASMs and advanced, precision-guided weapons, could the fighter be gaining an advantage in the battle with the heavier SAM? The main trend appears to be towards increasing the performance of lighter systems, increasing their lethal envelopes, making them more resistant to counter-measures and less reliant on active radar for target acquisition and tracking. Missiles will be faster, to reduce engagement times. Shorter-range weapons can also use passive means of detection, such as infra-red surveillance equipment, and low-probability-of-intercept guidance techniques such as laser beam-riding.

An example of the trends in smaller SAMs is the Oerlikon/Martin Marietta ADATS, a laser beam-riding weapon some 50 per cent faster than current missiles in its class. It shows how smaller missiles are more easily built into protected vehicles; a complete ADATS system can be mounted on a single armoured vehicle, with eight rounds ready to fire. It is also an interesting example of the flexibility that is being built into modern missile systems thanks to miniaturisation, optical guidance and other technologies. ADATS is designed to attack tanks as well as aircraft, and is light enough to be adapted to helicopter launch.

Medium-range SAMs will retain their value for the defence of fixed, high-value targets such as airfields. It is possible that some will go underground for protection, and be launched vertically from silos. Vertical launch has already been adopted by the Soviet and British navies, because of its advantages in rate of fire, all-round defence and mechanical redundancy.

The conventional missile will lose none of its importance to the land, sea or air battle, but it will be joined in increasing numbers by a new race of unmanned military air vehicles, falling somewhere between the traditional 'drone' or RPV and the missile itself. Currently, these UVSs are at a very early stage of their evolution. They are controversial in military circles, and often encounter opposition among air force commanders, virtually all of whom are ex-pilots. It is also argued that one of the main advantages of the UVS, cost, may diminish or disappear when the original concept is adapted into something of any military usefulness.

The term UVS is used, rather than RPV, because most of the new systems are not 'remotely piloted'. Instead, they are flown by their own pre-programmed navigation and flight control systems. Some of them can be commanded to change their destination in

flight, but they do not need a full-time pilot. Others have no means for human intervention at all.

High-performance UVSs were extensively used for reconnaissance during the Viet Nam war, but for a number of reasons, some political and some economic, their use was sharply reduced in the mid-1970s. (The Soviet Union still uses a Mach 2·8 reconnaissance UVS, and some covert US units may still maintain such systems on strength.) Most attention, though, has switched to far smaller, much less complicated machines. These saw their first use in combat in 1982, when the Israeli Defence Forces used Scout and Mastiff UVSs to reconnoitre Syrian SAM positions.

Reconnaissance is one of the prime roles for the UVS, and one in which it will be increasingly used. Barely bigger than a large bird or an enthusiast's flying model, the UVS is virtually impossible to shoot down, and yet it can carry a stabilised, steerable tv camera and transmission equipment and send instant tv images to the 'consumers' at the front of the battle. The next stage in development is represented by the US Army's Aquila, which will be developed with a night-reconnaissance capability, and carries a laser to mark targets for guided artillery shells. The British Phoenix system will perform a similar task. By the 1990s, reconnaissance UVSs will be established in service with most ground forces.

The main issue in the debate over the UVS is cost. The Israeli systems are inexpensive, but are designed for daytime reconnaissance in a not too intensive electronic environment, and require a flat road and a certain amount of piloting skill. Night-reconnaissance equipment is a reasonably cheap addition. Making the data-links proof against heavy jamming can be expensive, as can the provision of an automated, rough-terrain recovery system. The cost of Aquila has come in for criticism and future systems will be cheaper.

The second mission to be performed by an operational UVS is the suppression of hostile electronic warfare (EW) equipment. In 1983, the USAF unveiled an extraordinary machine called Pave Tiger. Many details of the system are classified, but it is known that Pave Tiger was developed in considerable haste, to deal with a new and very effective ground-based Soviet EW system.

Pave Tiger is based on the Boeing-developed Brave-200 airframe, weighing 250 pounds, injection-moulded in foam plastic and glass fibre, and powered by a cheap commercial piston engine driving a small plastic propeller. Fifteen of these 'air vehicles' can be stowed in separate cells in a module the size of a standard freight container, each attached to its individual launch rail. The module is attached to a standard power unit and a control box; the vehicles pop out of their cells

REMOTELY PILOTED VEHICLES

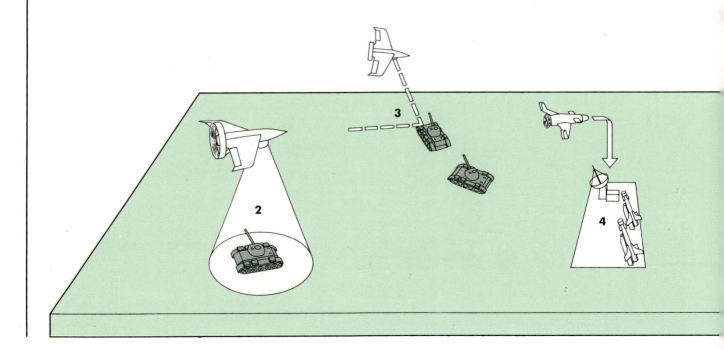

*A British contender in the low cost military drone stakes is the Frazer Nash RPV capable of being launched from the back of a Land Rover (**left**). Even more diminutive is the ML Sprite RPV helicopter (**above**) capable of carrying a TV camera or laser designator in its tiny airframe*

RPVs (also known as unmanned vehicle systems or UVS) have a wide range of roles on the automated battlefield. They can be used for reconnaissance both on the front line and deep within enemy territory (1), reporting either by returning with film capsules or by transmitting TV pictures in real time (2). They can be used as platforms for laser target designators (3) or as direct attack weapons themselves, homing for example on hostile air intercept radars (4). More subtly they can be used for electronic spoofing, their presence causing hostile radars to switch on allowing Elint platforms to glean the vital electronic intelligence necessary for a defence suppression campaign (5)

on demand and take off on a pre-programmed track, loaded before launch from the control unit.

Details of the mission and payload of Pave Tiger are classified, but it appears to be what is known as a 'harassment' system. A homing device picks up emissions from the system to be suppressed, and the vehicle, which carries an explosive charge, begins an attack run towards it. The operators respond by shutting down their transmissions. Instead of crashing like an ordinary missile, though, the UVS abandons its attack and begins to orbit the target, circling for hours and diving to the attack should the operators restart the system. One small drone can paralyse a highly sophisticated EW system for hours, at far less cost than the short-term suppression achieved by an airstrike.

Like many modern weapons, the Brave-200 can be adapted to different missions and targets by changing its guidance system and payload. Because the vehicle is cheap and standardised it can be built and used in large numbers. Similar devices could even carry PGSMs, making them more than just a nuisance.

Of all aerospace systems, satellites and UVSs will benefit the most from the development of artificial intelligence, and its implementation in lightweight VHSIC-based electronic equipment. While current UVSs can act according to sensor information, or according to a pre-programmed set of instructions, an 'intelligent' UVS will be able to do both at once. A future tactical reconnaissance UVS, for example, will be crossing country at high speed on a programmed track when its wide-angle, scanning infra-red sensor detects a vehicle. IR instantly cues long-focus optical and other sensors, and target-recognition identifies a tank. The UVS turns, returns to the same spot using its inertial reference system, and makes a low-altitude run over the tank's projected track, revealing the entire formation. The UVS memory tells it that the formation is very significant, and its datalink promptly transmits high-resolution images to an orbiting high-altitude relay UVS behind friendly lines.

Combining intelligence with immediate action, such a UVS will have become a true robot. Note that it does not require a human operator in such a high-risk situation; the reduced size of the unmanned vehicle further increases its chances of survival. Neither does it saturate the data-link with high-quality images of passing trees. The technology envisaged is not far from reality, but at present such data processing can only be combined with action in a 'stop-think-move' cycle. It may be very different in the 1990s.

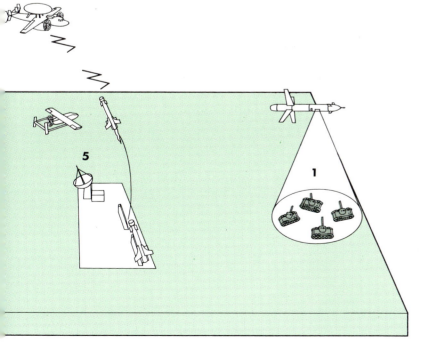

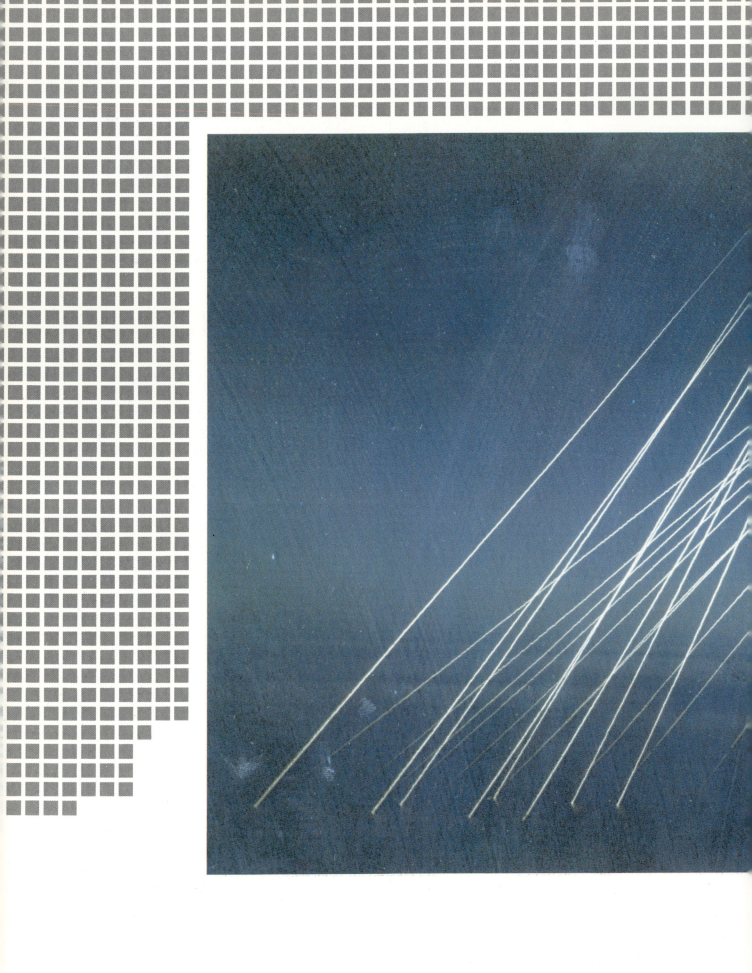

3 STRATEGIC NUCLEAR WEAPONS

'Ban the Bomb' has always been a misleading slogan, however admirable the aim behind it. The 'Bomb', that big scary shiny, metallic teardrop daubed by generations of political cartoonists with an 'H' for hydrogen, in reality is barely recognisable as a bomb at all. But 'Ban the Shell' or 'Ban the re-entry vehicle' perhaps do not have the same emotive alliterative power. Nuclear weapons have been packed into short-range tactical missiles, into air defence missiles, into artillery shells, into anti-submarine depth charges, into sea-skimming anti-ship missiles, into suitcase-sized demolition charges and into the awesomely destructive multiple warheads of intercontinental and submarine-based ballistic missiles. The free-fall gravity bomb of the sort that wiped out Hiroshima and Nagasaki is still in use by US strategic and NATO tactical air forces but, in terms of operational effectiveness, they might be considered as obsolete as the B-29 bombers that were the world's first nuclear weapon delivery systems.

Thermonuclear weapons are more than just very powerful explosive devices, but in understanding the technology of nuclear weapon systems it is worth distinguishing straight away between the weapon system itself and the means by which it reaches its target — the delivery system. The V-2 rocket for example, developed by the Germans during the Second World War, was a strategic delivery system but could carry no more than high explosive and bombard, at comparatively close-range, only area targets (the sprawling city of London) with woeful inaccuracy. Over 1000 V-2s fell on London loaded with a ton of high explosive each and killed less than one individual per missile. Two atom bombs dropped on Japan killed over a quarter of a million people.

This combination of unstoppable delivery system and weapon of mass destruction is the cornerstone of the doctrine of deterrence — that the offensive capacity of one side must be matched by reliable, survivable offensive weapons on the other, certain of retaliating even after their number has been decimated by a first strike. The technology of nuclear weapons therefore is not just about what makes them so awesomely destructive but about the delivery system that carries them, its reliability, its range, its accuracy, its performance — does it fly fast or slowly?, does it have single or multiple warheads?, its ability to get through and, very importantly, its ability to survive when its own base is under equivalent attack.

It is equally important to comprehend the network of Command, Control and Communication (C³) on which the doctrine of deterrence also depends.

Nuclear Weapons, Principles and Effects

The fission weapons so far constructed have used the isotopes U-235 or Pu-239 as the fissile material. To trigger a fission reaction it is necessary to put together a mass of these materials large enough to ensure that high energy neutron particles do not escape from its surface but strike other heavy atoms within the material, causing them in turn to release more neutrons and sustain the chain reaction. The minimum amount of material that will do this is called the critical mass. The critical mass of a sphere of Uranium 235 is approximately 52 kilograms. That of weapons grade Pu-239 is around ten kilograms while these can be further reduced by surrounding the fissile material with a reflective medium such as pure uranium to contain and bounce back neutrons which would otherwise escape.

The critical mass has to be brought and held together long enough for a chain reaction to occur but not before maximum supercriticality has been reached ('pre-initiation'). The reflector therefore is further designed to act as a 'tamper' to hold the materials together long enough. Two basic design techniques have been used to initiate a fission reaction and both were tested in the bombs dropped on Japan. The Hiroshima bomb used the 'gun assembly' technique in which two subcritical slugs of uranium were fired into each other down a 'gun barrel' using high explosive. The Nagasaki bomb, 'Fat Man', used high explosive 'lenses' surrounding a uranium tamper and hollow plutonium sphere, blasting the material inwards into a supercritical mass.

The very high energy generated by nuclear fission is enough to trigger its opposite — the fusion of light atoms into heavier ones. In 'thermonuclear' weapons, the heavier isotopes of hydrogen, dueterium and lithium are fused into helium. Both are gases at normal temperatures so in some applications lithium 6-dueteride, a solid at normal temperatures, is used as the thermonuclear fuel, the necessary trilium being bred during detonation by the neutron bombardment of the lithium 6.

By incorporating such 'thermonuclear' fuels into a fission bomb, its yield is greatly increased by the large number of extra neutrons produced in the fusion reaction which in turn produces additional fission in the weapon's own fissile material (these are known as thermonuclear boosted fission weapons). Alternatively the detonation of the primary fissile core can compress and ignite a separate 'secondary' component containing fusion materials, and in turn this could be transferred to a third stage and so on, in

The technological development that has driven the procurement patterns of nuclear weapons and the making of nuclear strategy above all in the past twenty years has been the ever greater accuracy achievable over ever longer ranges made possible by computerised guidance systems. In mathematical terms this is expressed as the 'Circular Error of Probability' defined as the radius of a circle in which will land half of the rounds aimed at it. The longer a ballistic missile's range, the greater will be its CEP.

A multi-stage ballistic missile uses large amounts of chemical energy in its boost phase to take its payload into space where the post-boost vehicle (PBV) acts as a miniature spacecraft controlling the re-entry pattern of the multiple independently targeted re-entry vehicles (MIRVs).

Cruise missiles in contrast fly through the atmosphere under continuous power using wings for lift, navigating by such techniques as terrain contour matching (TERCOM), an onboard computer comparing the radar return of the landscape over which it is flying with a pre-set digital map

MISSILE FLIGHT PROFILES

Circular error of probability

Range and accuracy

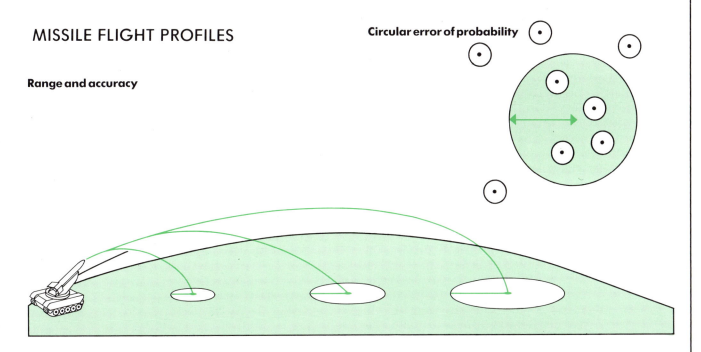

Multi-stage ballistic missile

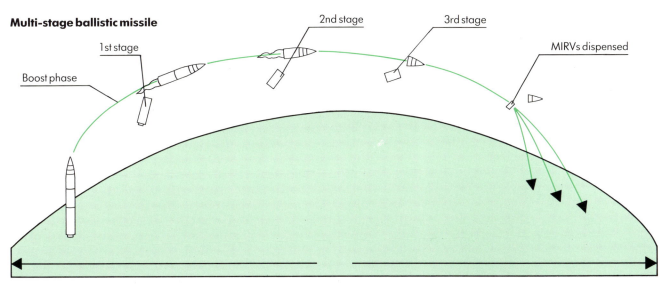

Boost phase

1st stage

2nd stage

3rd stage

MIRVs dispensed

Cruise missile

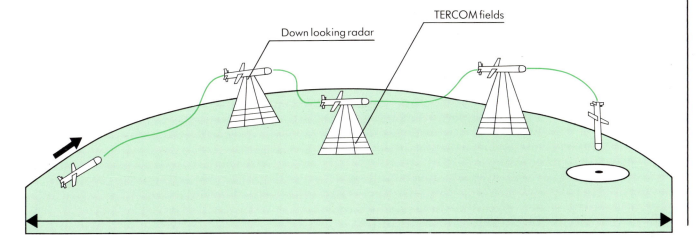

Down looking radar

TERCOM fields

theory there is no limit to the yield of fusion weapons.

Each stage will contribute to the total energy released by a thermonuclear weapon with varying balances of the fission to fusion yield ('yield' is shorthand for the energy released in the explosion measured in kilotons and megatons, respectively the explosive equivalent of one thousand and one million tons of trinitrotoluene chemical high explosive).

Some currently operational weapons feature 'variable yields' allowing, on paper at least, some operational flexibility in battlefield use. In fission weapons yields could tech-

nically be made variable by altering the sequencing of the chain reaction initiation. In boosted-fission weapons, the yield could be varied by feeding selected amounts of tritium gas into the fissile core from an external source. The same technique could be used in thermonuclear weapons with primary and secondary stages. Some earlier 'selectable yield' weapons have interchangeable fissile cores.

'Warhead' is a loose term which may be defined as that part of the weapon system which contains the destructive element. In the case of nuclear weapons the warhead will be associated with highly sophisticated fuzing

Land based intercontinental ballistic missiles (ICBMs) in the past have had greater range, payload and accuracy than their submarine based equivalents. They present a problem in that being emplaced in fixed site silos they are vulnerable to a first strike, yet because they are powerful and accurate, they are themselves militarily useful as first strike weapons. **Left:** Titan II silo venting moments before launch.

Right: Female Strategic Air Command officer checks a launch control panel.

Below: Minuteman III test launch

and arming devices to protect them from accidental or malicious release. The basis is the 'voting' principle which requires simultaneous actions by two or more authorised individuals to commence the arming of a nuclear weapon by gaining access to release codes. These in turn are fed into Permissive Action Links (PALs) which act as super-sophisticated versions of high street cash dispensers, requiring a preset sequence of digits to unlock the arming circuits and offering only a 'limited try' to incorrect entries before locking permanently. Other systems include code-activated override mechanisms and protection from shock and electrical surges. New generation US weapons such as cruise missile warheads contain high explosive triggers made of especially stable material, claimed to be immune to accidental detonation or accident.

The Effect of Nuclear Weapons

The immediate effects of a nuclear explosion are heat, blast and ionising radiation released in proportions dependent on the type of weapon and where it was exploded, in the air, on the ground or under water for example. In an air burst, roughly half the energy would be released as blast, a third as heat and the rest as radiation, both 'prompt', that is released immediately and long-term, as fall-out.

The heat flash travels out fastest from the centre of detonation as X-rays are absorbed by the surrounding air and progressively re-radiated on longer wavelengths forming the characteristic luminous mass of air or 'fireball' which grows and rises.

The blast front from an airburst travels out in two spheres, one being an echo from the ground, merging in a so-called 'Mach front' which may have an overpressure double that of the original blast front. (Overpressure is the degree of pressure greater than that of the atmosphere, negative overpressure is encountered behind the advancing blast front which brings its own implosive destructive effects while hurricane winds will rage inwards after the initial blast wave has passed, drawn in by the chimney effect of the rising fireball.)

A nuclear detonation will release immediate or 'prompt' radiation, again depending on the type of weapon and circumstances, producing neutrons, X-rays, gamma rays, and alpha and beta particles. Neutron bombardment is the most deadly to human tissue but neutrons do not travel as far as gamma particles. The amount of gamma radiation in turn falls off according to the square of the distance from the source, combined with the absorption effects of the material through which it travels. The amount of radiation however falls off much faster with distance than do the blast and heat effects. The detonation of a one-megaton thermonuclear weapon would produce a dose of 200 000 rads to a human being one kilometre distant, but at two kilometres that has fallen to 700 rads (remembering that a total skin dose of 450 rads would be lethal to 50 per cent of normal healthy adults). However this lethal radius is the same as for the other deadly effects of the notional one-megaton airburst, a person in the way would be killed three times over, but for smaller weapons the reverse is true — the ratio of radiation to blast and heat becomes greater as the size of the yield drops. This is the principle behind the so called 'neutron bomb'.

The blast and heat effects of a nuclear weapon may be devastating against cities and appallingly destructive in densely populated areas such as extensive tracts of West Germany but are less so against hardened point targets such as missile silos or mobile dispersed targets such as armoured formations. The 'neutron bomb' (not a bomb at all but a shell or missile warhead) is designed to attack the flesh and blood occupants inside armour, for example by maximising the lethal effects of high energy neutrons. These are produced by the fusion of deuterium and tritium, keeping the fission yield as small as possible. Each reaction of a deuterium with a tritium nucleus releases a neutron charged with 14 million electron volts (14MeV), in quantities six times more numerous than that relayed by a fission chain reaction. A neutron or 'enhanced radia-

tion' weapon will release 30 per cent of its energy as prompt radiation compared with a 'standard' low yield fission weapon's five per cent. The military argument for enhanced radiation weapons sees them as a means of attacking massed armour without the 'collateral damage' caused by standard battlefield nuclear weapons.

A nuclear explosion releases a range of radioactive isotopes — altogether some 300 different radioactive products are produced in fission with half lives ranging from fractions of seconds to millions of years. (The half life of a radioactive substance is the time required for its level of radioactivity to decay by one half but, as a general rule, the radiation level following a nuclear explosion will decay at the rate t-1·2 where t equals time. For every sevenfold elapse in time therefore, the radioactivity will fall away by ten.)

As the rising cloud of dust and ash produced by a nuclear explosion begins to cool, stable fission isotopes begin to condense on the particles, and these will fall back to earth according to wind and weather conditions and their size. Finer particles will climb into the troposphere and beyond, falling out over weeks and months according to global climatic conditions. In an all-out war this irradiated debris would join the darkening aerosol thrown up by other explosions, by the ash and smoke from blazing cities, oil storage and forest fires which might climb into the atmosphere to blot out sunlight for months on end.

Weapon Systems

Military considerations do not recognise the 'doomsday' aspect of nuclear weapons. They are about targets which, although they might be cities teaming with millions of people are also missile silos and underground command centres which require enormous destructive force to root them out. The effective destructive power of any weapon, whether a slingshot or an atomic bomb, is a function of its accuracy of delivery, reliability and energy yield. But the destructive power of an explosive increases by the cube root of the yield — a one-megaton weapon does not have destructive effects one thousand times greater than a one-kiloton weapon. Technological efforts have concentrated not on increasing the yield (in fact the reverse is true) but on *accuracy* and *survivability*. These have nothing to do with the nuclear weapon itself but rather with the system which carries it and the method of its basing.

Accuracy and Counterforce

In order to destroy a hardened military target such as an ICBM silo, sufficient blast over-

COUNTERFORCE AND ACCURACY

ICBM

Decreasing CEPs means that the kind of target that can be brought under threat itself changes. First generation ICBMs had single warheads but enough accuracy to target rival weapons as well as cities. This is called 'counterforce' as opposed to 'countervalue' targeting. The development of MIRVs meanwhile meant that a single missile could knock out several of its rivals at once, thus increasing the imperative for a first strike

MIRVs dispensed

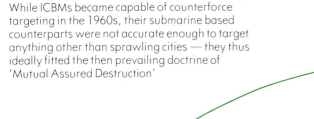

ICBM silos

First Generation SLBM

While ICBMs became capable of counterforce targeting in the 1960s, their submarine based counterparts were not accurate enough to target anything other than sprawling cities — they thus ideally fitted the then prevailing doctrine of 'Mutual Assured Destruction'

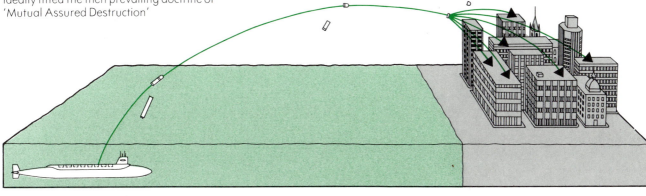

Third Generation SLBM

Developments in guidance systems mean that submarine-launched missiles such as Trident have the accuracy to be considered counterforce weapons. Trident II will use global positioning satellites for mid-course guidance and carry a large number of MIRVs

Global Positioning Satellite

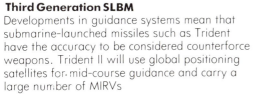

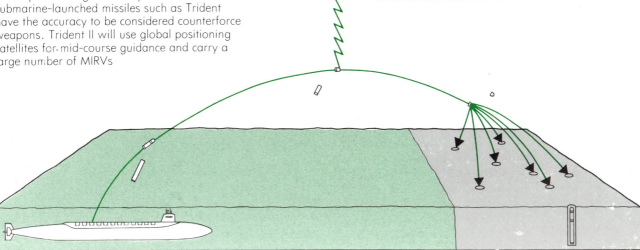

pressure must be delivered to pulverise thousands of tons of ferro-concrete. This may mean using more than one warhead but the basis of such 'counterforce' targeting (counterforce means attacking the weapons of your opponent rather than 'countervalue' targets such as cities) is both accuracy of delivery and accuracy of fixing the target's real position derived from satellite mapping.

For almost two decades the idea of 'mutual assured destruction' (MAD) underpinned the doctrine of deterrence. It was argued that nuclear weapons were so destructive even the exchange of relatively small numbers would surely destroy both sides in an all-out nuclear war. But because delivery systems were relatively inaccurate, the side which struck first could never entirely eliminate the weapons of retaliation which would surely fall on its cities. The 1960s vintage submarine-based Polaris missiles, for example, were ideal MAD-weapons, out of reach from a first strike and yet not accurate enough themselves to target anything other than sprawling cities, but certainly accurate enough to be sure of wiping them out. Land-based ICBMs however were a different matter. Because they were land based and had a fixed launch point they had both a greater degree of accuracy than sea-based missiles and in turn presented temptingly fixed targets to their rivals.

It was the rise of the Soviet ICBM force in the 1970s that chipped away at MAD and eventually buried it. The existence of a very powerful and accurate Soviet land-based missile force with multiple warheads, it was argued, opened a 'window of vulnerability' which gravely imperilled the United States. A proportion of these ICBMs could be used to eliminate the land-based leg of the US strategic triad, the Minuteman ICBMs, by attacking with MIRVs. The hydra-headed ICBMs could target more silos with multiple warheads than missiles actually launched, leaving a proportion in reserve to threaten an equally devastating second strike. The US supreme commander would only have a single option — that of attacking Soviet cities with the surviving submarine-based missiles and thus inviting the destruction of US cities by the remainder of the enemy missile force in return. That option was closed and thus the US would 'lose' a nuclear war with the destruction of the strategic warfighting element — the ICBMs.

Even that scenario is history with the adoption in the US during the last year of the Carter administration of a deterrent doctrine based on counterforce rather than MAD (Presidential Directive 59) and the implementation under the Reagan administration of a vast strategic weapons procurement pro-

gramme which, in the type of new systems deployed, blurs the old distinction between the big, accurate ICBMs and the cities-only inaccurate SLBMs.

Three Studies in Accuracy, Pershing II, Tomahawk GLCM, Trident

In the first years of the 1980s the US Army, Air Force and Navy deployed systems which incorporated the technological revolution in accuracy achieved experimentally in the 1970s. Each in its own way illustrates the twists that technology adds to the already complex coils of deterrence, and deserves a closer look.

The US Army's Pershing II intermediate range ballistic missile became operational in Europe at the end of 1983. Along with the arrival of the first two flights of ground-launched cruise missiles (GLCMs) at RAF Greenham Common, this represented the end of the beginning of the long process begun by NATO in 1979 known as Theatre Nuclear Force (TNF) modernisation.

At the end of 1983 there were one hundred and eight Pershing Is deployed in West Ger-

Above: *Prototype MX Peacekeeper ICBM fired from a test stand. Originally designed to be deployed in vast underground shelters within which it would be shuttled around, after a long political battle some 50 or so Peacekeepers will be deployed in fixed site silos*

Right: *A Trident I SLBM breaks surface. Trident I is a three-stage submarine-launched ballistic missile with a range of 7400 km. The follow on Trident II will have greater range, but even more importantly, accuracy consistent with a land-based counterpart*

many. The Pershing I, which the Pershing II is set to replace on a one-for-one basis, is the only US Army nuclear system aimed at preset targets deep in Warsaw Pact territory and forms part of SACEUR's (Supreme Allied Commander Europe) QRA (Quick Reaction Alert) forces kept at permanent readiness according to a three-stage 'Force Generation' level.

The Pershing Ia (which superseded the Pershing I in the early 1970s, the upgrades confined to the mobility of the fire support units and the ability to operate from unsurveyed firing positions) has a range of up to 740 kilometres and uses an inertial guidance system to achieve accuracies of 400 metres circular error probability (CEP) at maximum range. The warhead is the W50 with selectable yields of 60, 200 and 400 kilotons.

Pershing II in fact has a warhead (the W85 based on a new generation free-fall bomb) with a much smaller yield than the weapon which it is replacing, reportedly selectable from single- to 20-kiloton yield. It has however a far longer reach, variously quoted as between 1300 and 1800 kilometres, flies extremely fast (eight times the speed of sound in the boost phase) and is far more accurate than the system it replaces.

Pershing II is a ballistic missile with a radar guidance system in its nose. The guidance system developed by Goodyear Aerospace and Norden Systems is called Radar Area Correlation (RADAG). In the terminal descent phase, the radar activates scanning, at 120 rpm, an initial reference area and comparing the return with a pre-stored reference map. Guidance commands are generated and transmitted as course corrections to the re-entry vehicle's control vanes.

The result is a reduction of CEP to under 50 metres and over ranges which, from launch in West Germany, bring targets deep within the western Soviet Union under the Pershing's thrall.

This, allied to the weapon's very short flight time, is why the Pershings in particular were seen by the Soviets as especially menacing and such stumbling blocks in the Geneva intermediate range nuclear weapons talks which collapsed at the end of 1983. Speaking in 1979 in Congressional testimony the US Secretary of the Army, Clifford L Alexander, gave a glimpse at targeting policy for the new generation weapons — potential Pershing II targets include hardened and soft missile sites, airfields, naval bases, nuclear, biological and chemical storage sites, command and control centres, headquarters, rail yards, road networks, choke points, ammunition and petroleum storage, troop concen-

trations and dams/locks. Pershing II is particularly effective against hard point and underground targets because of its high accuracy and the unique earth penetrator warhead capability.

The accuracy and range of the Pershing II, in spite of the far smaller yield warhead, considerably raised the temperature of arms control diplomacy. The fact that it was seen by NATO as a counterdeployment to the Soviet SS-20, itself a highly sophisticated theatre range missile with a triple independently targetable warhead, did little to soothe Europe's nuclear jitters during the run up to and aftermath of the initial deployment.

The ground-launched cruise missile is another essay in accuracy. It is a US Air Force system, like Pershing part of the NATO intermediate nuclear force (INF) modernisation programme with a total of 464 due to be for-

Below: *Technical checks in progress on a ground-launched cruise missile (GLCM) flight, inside Greenham Common airbase for long the focus of protest against NATO's 1979 theatre nuclear force modernisation decision. In the background is the trailer/erector/launcher (TEL) vehicle*

ward deployed at six main operating bases in Europe. A 'cruise' missile flies through the air using wings for lift and a small air-breathing turbofan engine for propulsion — flying in fact at the speed of a jet airliner, far slower than the Pershing's Mach 8. But what it lacks in speed it makes up in numbers and in accuracy, again showing the results of the targeting revolution made possible by satellite mapping and onboard computer power, in being able to 'snipe' at critical point targets over long ranges delivering a nuclear weapon with devastating accuracy. The disadvantages are the same as those which might affect the penetrating bomber which cruise technology goes some way to supersede. They are vulnerable to counter-air defences such as surface-to-air missiles and interceptor aircraft armed with look down, shoot down air-to-air missiles. US cruise missiles in their ground-, sea- and air-launched varieties use a guidance technique called TERCOM — 'terrain' contour matching. Like the Pershing's system, it uses a hybrid of inertial navigation and computer analysis of geographical information but TERCOM sustains the process over far greater distances taking

Below: GLCM test launch from the TEL

Below Bottom: Pershing II test launch. In contrast to cruise the Pershing has a very short flight time flying at speeds eight times that of sound. A radar ground mapper in the nose makes it highly accurate

multiple readings along the approach route to its target.

The system uses a down-looking radar altimeter to measure height above ground allied to an altimeter reading atmospheric pressure and thus height above an absolute datum such as sea level. The difference between these two readings provides a measure of the height of the ground surveyed below. The reading obtained is the average for 1500 square metres of land. By taking repeated readings, the digital results can be compared by the guidance computer with a preset matrix of the approach route, the necessary information already obtained by satellite reconnaissance and turned into numbers inside the guidance computer. By comparing the measured track with all possible similar tracks in the matrix, any along-track or cross-track deviations can be corrected.

At the other end of the spectrum is the Trident submarine-launched ballistic missile system. Trident I missiles became operational with the US Navy in 1970 and the Trident II is scheduled to enter US service by 1988 and the British Royal Navy sometime thereafter.

Trident I is the third generation of American SLBMs, following on from the 1960s vintage Polaris and Poseidon missiles originally developed to be the assured destruction component of the strategic triad. Submarine-launched missiles were not as accurate as their land-based counterparts or penetrating bombers so they could only be targeted with certainty against 'countervalue' area targets. But because once out at sea they themselves were invulnerable to a first strike they ideally suited the mutual assured destruction deterrent philosophies of the time.

Poseidon doubled the accuracy of the original Polaris and introduced multiple independently targetable warheads carrying fourteen re-entry vehicles (RVs).

Trident I is a three-stage missile with greater range than Poseidon (7400 compared with 4500 kilometres) which greatly increases the operational flexibility of the launching submarine because it has far more sea room in which to patrol yet still hold its targets in range. At the same time accuracy remains akin to that of Poseidon even at the greater ranges because Trident I introduces the sophistication of stellar sighting into the all-inertial navigation of the earlier generation system.

Inertial navigation is a fundamental principle of missile guidance which techniques such as Radag, Tercom and stellar sighting merely fine tune. At the heart of an inertial navigation system (INS) is an array of gyroscopes and accelerometers integrated with highly accurate timekeeping. By knowing 'where it started from' the system can record changes in attitude, direction, acceleration and velocity and generate guidance commands to steer the missile towards the preset target. As far as land-based missiles are concerned, the start point is fixed and INS guidance is practical and effective over long ranges. Land-mobile and sea-launched missiles need a reference imparted before launch — SLBMs get it from the submarine's own inertial guidance system (SINS — the US Navy Ships Inertial Navigation system) fed into the missiles' computer before launch by the fire-control computer. The US Peacekeeper ICBM, originally designed to be land mobile, is equipped with the so-called AIRS system (Advanced Inertial Reference Sphere) which would allow missiles to be shuttled about without needing fresh location determination each time.

Every time one navigation system hands over to another, there is a degradation in accuracy. The launch submarine's SINS for example hands over to the missile's own inertial navigation system, whose function is to direct the flight in its boost phase as the payload is accelerated to the correct velocity in the correct ballistic trajectory. In a MIRV

missile that payload is a small space vehicle called the Post Boost Vehicle (PBV) or 'bus'. The PBV has its own attitude control motor and guidance system allowing it to depart from the original ballistic trajectory, dispensing its cargo of nuclear armed re-entry vehicles over a pre-set 'footprint' of targets. Because the PBV takes its reference from that established in the boost phase, any errors in the system will be cumulative and this is why first generation multiple warhead systems were not as accurate as the single warhead systems they replaced. Trident I's PBV however, is fitted with the Mk 5 stellar inertial guidance system which takes a star shot of the heavens, using these celestial references to update, fine tune and correct its course. Trident II with even greater range will also use the Navstar Global Positioning system, an interlocking lattice of satellites, to fix its true position. Trident II is designed to afford the US with 'second strike counterforce potential', that is it matches the 1980s doctrines of counterforce and nuclear war fighting rather than deterrence pure and simple because it has all the accuracy and 'hard target kill capability' of a land-based missile, yet it is itself immune to a first strike.

US developed cruise missiles come in three varieties — land-, air- and sea-launched. As such they can be said to impart long range strategic nuclear strike power to the humblest of launch platforms (in GLCM's case, an articulated truck). Sea-launched cruise missiles (SLCMs) are destined to be installed on surface and sub-surface units of the US fleet ranging from the re-conditioned battleships of the Iowa class, to destroyers

Left: *The USS New Jersey fires a Tomahawk SLCM.*
Above: *An SLCM launched from a submerged US Navy attack submarine*

STRATEGIC COMMAND AND CONTROL

The efficiency and ability to survive of strategic command and control systems are as vital a component of nuclear forces as the weapons themselves and the bedrock of the idea of deterrence. Deterrence relies on the notion of assured retaliation, the decision making head must survive or at least authority to launch a retaliatory nuclear strike should be delegated to a pre-ordained chain of command, and the means by which authorised orders reach dispersed nuclear forces should also be resistant to an attack and function during and after such an attack.

That in itself requires warning, not so that defensive forces can be brought to bear (they do not exist) but so that plans for retaliation can be authorised and put into effect before the command system or indeed the weapons themselves can be destroyed. For the United States warning begins with geostationary satellites positioned to watch Soviet missile fields where the infra-red trace of a rocket in its boost phase would give the first indication of an ICBM launch.

The network of ballistic missile early warning radars (BMEWS) watch approach routes across the Arctic while the Pave Paws phased array sites monitor the United States eastern and western seaboards for submarine-launched missiles breaking

surface. The Soviet Union has a parallel network of missile warning radars plus a first generation ballistic missile defence (BMD) system guarding Moscow plus a massive SAM and interceptor air defence system.

Early warning is one component. The rest is Command and Control, the networks which animate and inform strategic nuclear forces. Much of it is satellite based (see Chapter 7) but much effort is going into land based systems using fibre-optic cables resistant to the effects of electromagnetic pulse (EMP) associated with nuclear detonations which would burn out conventional electronic equipment.

Above: *The huge phased array radar at Otis AFB Maryland codenamed Pave Paws watches the north eastern seaboard of the USA for submarine launched ballistic missiles breaking surface. The amount of warning time it could realise would be a matter of minutes. . . . by which time the President of the United States or his designated successor should be airborne in the E-4B National Emergency Airborne Command Post (**left**) able to communicate with US strategic land based and submarine based missile forces. The hump behind the cockpit contains a satellite communications aerial*

Below: *One of the systems via which the E-4B would transmit orders would be EC-130G Hercules TACAMO aircraft designed to communicate with ballistic missile firing submarines via 10 km long trailing aerials*

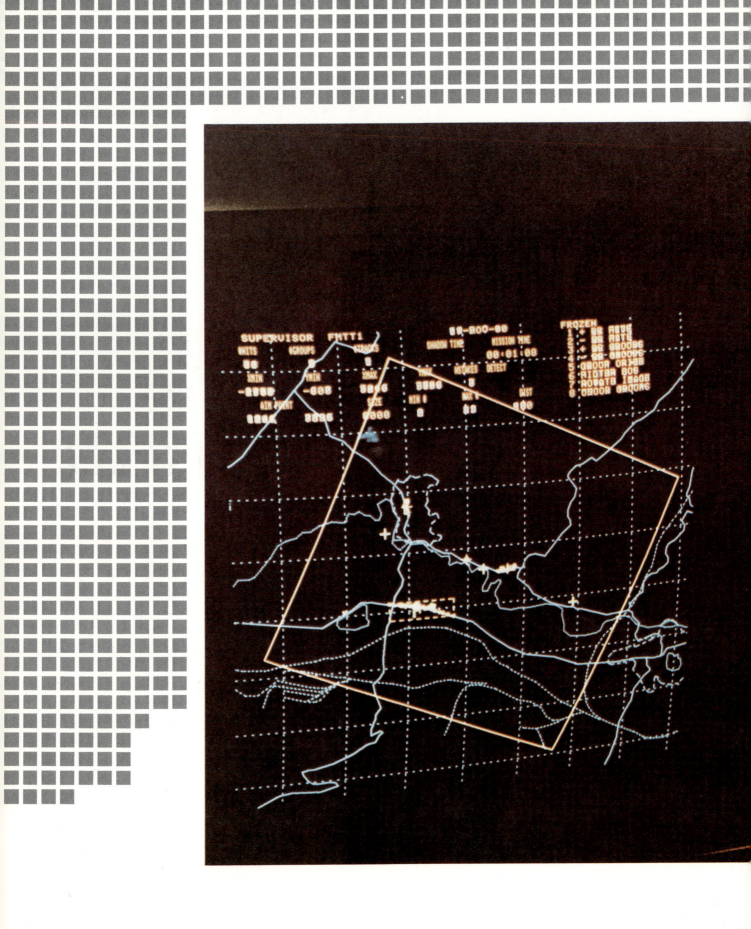

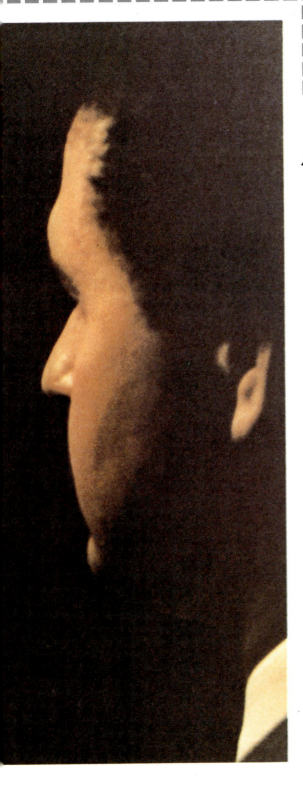

4 BEYOND THE NUCLEAR BATTLEFIELD

The systems described in the preceding chapter are strategic weapons, designed to fly over very long ranges and make attacks on the enemy heartland. Cruise missiles, in their land-, air- and sea-launched varieties blur the distinction between 'strategic and theatre' systems operating over 'intermediate' ranges of 1000 kilometres plus.

Both are distinct from battlefield nuclear weapons designed for use at short range against enemy military forces in the field or at sea.

The development of 'tactical' nuclear weapons and short range delivery systems followed rapidly on that of the first atomic bombs themselves. The availability of fissile material also greatly increased to match the demands for more and more applications as the US Army and Navy pressed to get in on the Air Force's nuclear monopoly.

The first tactical nuclear weapons were free-fall bombs delivered by fighter-bomber aircraft. In 1952 the US Army deployed an enormous 'atomic cannon' firing a 280 mm projectile which was the first non-aircraft delivered nuclear weapon. Through the 1950s these freakish and unwieldy nuclear projectiles were engineered for 8-inch and 155 mm artillery, for demolition munitions (land mines) and for short-range missiles such as Honest John or the extraordinary jeep-mounted Davy Crockett whose blast radius was greater than its range. The US Navy too went nuclear with the development of an extraordinary nuclear shell for battleship guns, bombs for carrier aircraft, anti-submarine depth bombs and rockets and nuclear-tipped air defence missiles.

A nuclear warhead was also considered appropriate for Air Force and Army air defence missiles such as the USAF's Genie and Nuclear Falcon air-to-air missiles, designed to blast bomber formations out of the sky, and the surface-to-air long range Bomarc and Nike-Hercules missiles.

With US tactical nuclear weapons forward deployed in Europe and in South Korea, the Soviet Union laboured to catch up at this level deploying, through the 1960s, free-fall bombs delivered by Frontal Aviation strike aircraft and systems such as the comparatively crude FROG (Free Rocket Over Ground) series, the SS-1 Scud heavy artillery rockets and the intermediate range SS-12.

This fact represented a difference in NATO and Soviet philosophies, the US concentrating on 'dual capable' systems (an artillery piece for example, firing either conventional or nuclear shells) and the Soviets on nuclear-only, highly mobile surface-to-surface rockets which were powerful but inaccurate, structuring their forces with conventional and

nuclear forces which best complemented each other on a battlefield which could be nuclear dominated from the start. In the 1970s however, the Soviets deployed nuclear artillery, even mortars, and gave the previously largely defensively postured Frontal Aviation a considerable nuclear strike capability.

All this put further pressure on NATO's doctrine of flexible response and the doctrine of 'first use'. Faced with Warsaw Pact predominance in conventional military power, and particularly in armour, NATO had still to take resort in tactical nuclear weapons with an openly articulated deterrent policy centred on their first use — if a Soviet attack proved unstoppable by conventional means, then it would be stopped by the first use of tactical nuclear weapons if necessary. The immediate problems lie in the highly complex and time consuming release procedures

Right: *The dual capable Lance missile serves with the US Army and several other NATO armies, the nuclear warheads kept under 'dual key' control*

Right below: *The M110 self propelled howitzer (here seen in British Army service) can hurl an 8-inch nuclear shell over 21 km*

Below: *The Soviets have concentrated on missiles rather than dual capable artillery as primary tactical nuclear delivery systems. The Scud A shown here is comparatively inaccurate but with a large warhead*

that are necessary to cut political authority into a decision making process that, at the front line at least, would be driven by military urgency. Second is the problem of nuclear weapon storage at forward sites with the need to concentrate them in a few high security areas which may be secure against terrorist attack but not against a nuclear or special force pre-emptive strike. These problems pale against that of escalation and trying to control a 'limited' use of nuclear weapons.

NATO's basic plan for the employment of tactical (and theatre) weapons is called the Nuclear Operations Plan (NOP) which also embraces theatre systems, air delivered weapons, Pershing II and cruise missiles and a number of submarine-based Poseidon warheads assigned to NOP targets. As far as tactical nuclear weapons are concerned, they would not be employed at the whim of a commander but released as pre-determined packages. A 'package' is defined as 'a group of nuclear weapons of specified yields for employment in a specified area within a limited time frame to support a tactical contingency'. Such packages could range from a relatively small number of artillery shells to a

The Multiple Launch Rocket System ripple-firing a twelve-rocket salvo

'Corps Package' consisting of up to 200 weapons depending on threat, mission, terrain and population characteristics.

In spite of the doctrine of flexible response it can be assumed that once the 'caps were popped' on even a few of NATO's battlefield weapons, escalation would be furious and devastating — that if the need arose to conduct a forward defence of West Germany against an overwhelmingly powerful conventional Soviet attack, a large proportion of the 'tactical' weapons assigned to the Nuclear Operations Plan would be used for striking deep into Warsaw Pact territory and the western Soviet Union, inviting the use of the strategic arsenals of both sides and all-out nuclear war. Because tactical nuclear weapons when used defensively might not only blast a large chunk of Central Europe into irradiated rubble but also surely invite a global holocaust, they have been seen by some strategists as a kind of self-made booby trap — their use is not credible politically or militarily and thus they fail as a deterrent.

Further, holding back dual capable systems such as fighter-bomber aircraft for a nuclear strike role dilutes the availability of conventional systems, as does the need to guard stockpiled nuclear warheads.

There remains a problem. The existence of tactical nuclear weapons is a comment on the West's existing plans to mount a conventional defence because of the 'holding under threat' factor. Short range missiles such as the US Army's Lance were deliberately engineered with a ten-kiloton fission warhead considered the optimum for forcing the dispersal of enemy armour, and denying an aggressor the chance to concentrate enough strength to force a breakthrough against a defence line, for the time being at least, held by conventional weapons such as anti-tank missiles and artillery.

Faced with the prospect of operations on a nuclear dominated battlefield, the Soviets in fact kept the emphasis on large numbers of tanks, prizing them for their mass and the certain amount of protection they afforded against radiation (in fact the kill radius for a ten-kiloton Lance warhead on tanks is 350 metres, crews would die at double this distance).

The Soviets further developed the doctrine of 'echeloning' military formations in staggered waves up to three and even four deep. NATO has expressed a certain confidence in being able to halt the first such wave by conventional means but after that the position is far bleaker — the 'Follow On Formations' would slam into the depleted defences where the first wave had burned out, overwhelming them with massive conventional firepower.

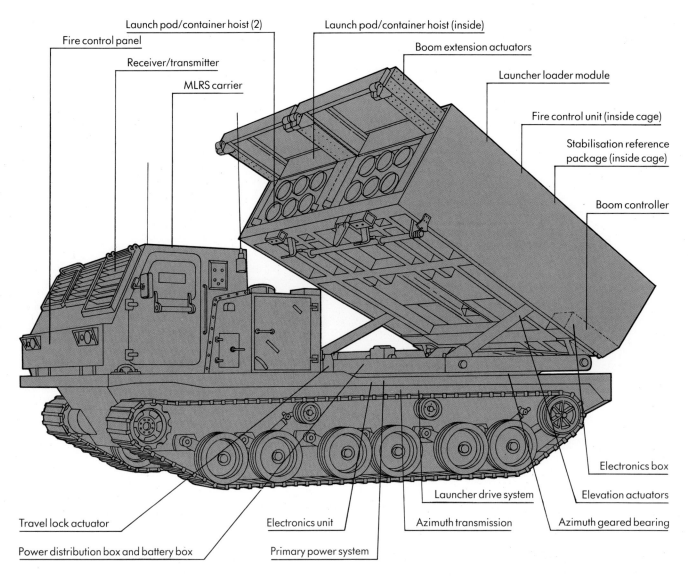

Fire control panel

Launch pod/container hoist (2)

Launch pod/container hoist (inside)

Boom extension actuators

Receiver/transmitter

Launcher loader module

MLRS carrier

Fire control unit (inside cage)

Stabilisation reference package (inside cage)

Boom controller

Electronics box

Elevation actuators

Azimuth geared bearing

Launcher drive system

Azimuth transmission

Electronics unit

Primary power system

Travel lock actuator

Power distribution box and battery box

MULTIPLE LAUNCH ROCKET SYSTEM

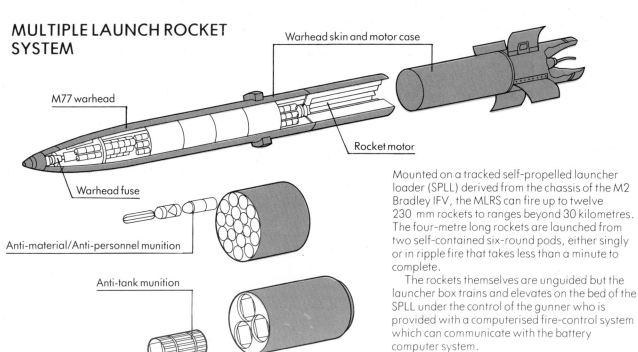

Warhead skin and motor case

M77 warhead

Rocket motor

Warhead fuse

Anti-material/Anti-personnel munition

Anti-tank munition

Mounted on a tracked self-propelled launcher loader (SPLL) derived from the chassis of the M2 Bradley IFV, the MLRS can fire up to twelve 230 mm rockets to ranges beyond 30 kilometres. The four-metre long rockets are launched from two self-contained six-round pods, either singly or in ripple fire that takes less than a minute to complete.

The rockets themselves are unguided but the launcher box trains and elevates on the bed of the SPLL under the control of the gunner who is provided with a computerised fire-control system which can communicate with the battery computer system.

Emerging Technology and Follow On Formation Attack

The Warsaw Pact's numerical superiority in armour and artillery (three to one) presents NATO with more than just a problem of numbers. Because of the accidents of history the boundary of confrontation is set along the line which bisected Germany in 1945, no natural barriers, rivers or mountain ranges mark the frontier where the two massively armed challengers meet. NATO is politically bound to a doctrine of forward defence, of meeting an attack close to the frontier and not trading ground and taking up a defence on the River Rhine for example. The forward defence strategy however, invites the Warsaw Pact to go for a quick victory and makes more urgent the early, if not the first, use of tactical nuclear weapons.

The second factor is airpower where the Warsaw Pact enjoys a superiority of two to one. Any counter-air war in Europe would not be a matter of gallant one-to-one dogfights but a deadly game in which the opening moves would be critical — massive strikes on each sides' main and secondary operating bases, striving to catch enemy airpower refuelling and rearming on the ground where it is most vulnerable, or at least to deny it the runways and stores for effective operations. Equally vital 'counter-air' targets would be ground radars and airborne early warning systems without which effective air defence would dissolve into fragments.

The problems of forward defence and deep strike counter-air warfare both open themselves to solutions by new or 'emerging' technology (ET) which has caused some radical rethinking of NATO's deterrent posture in Europe. ET has moved from the laboratories into experimental and operational weapon systems. The arguments continue as to how best to forge technological sophistication into a shield which is effective both militarily and politically.

About the New Technology

Electronics and 'information technology' are revolutionising military considerations as so much else. It is not just the substitution of machine for human intelligence but the far greater and inexhaustible capacity of machine intelligence for performing certain military tasks which is forcing the pace of change. A look at the integrated technologies of target surveillance, acquisition and target designation will illustrate how.

Virtually anyone or anything of military intent, whether it is a barefoot guerilla fighter pushing a bicycle through a jungle trail or an armoured division on the move, will have a set of 'signatures' — sound, visual, temperature, shape, size, chemical emissions, electromagnetic emissions, radar cross-sections and so-on. The oldest priority in warfare is to find where the enemy is, ascertain the hostile intent and, if possible, prevent it from being carried out but today, instead of relying on brain, eye and muscle, that task is carried out by automated sensors allied to computer power. Whether that sensor/computer package is represented by a huge network of air defence radars or in the homing head of a 'smart' missile, the principle is the same, instead of relying on human judgement to distinguish friend from foe and aim the weapon, machine intelligence will read the target's signatures and either because it has already been told that that particular source of electromagnetic returns is hostile, or because it has its own onboard intelligence able to make discretionary judgements, it should now unerringly fulfil its destructive mission.

In the age of precision guidance and robotic delivery systems, the distinction between weapon platform (the ship, vehicle or aircraft which carries it) and weapon system is increasing with the balance tilting against the platform. A penetrating strike aircraft for example is now so laden down with technology and self defence systems to allow platform and pilot to get through defended airspace and back, that its actual offensive load of conventional munitions gets less and less significant. Meanwhile they consume ever more resources — the Royal Air Force's Tornado GR 1 for example, designed for the deep strike, interdiction and anti-airfield role, comes at a price tag of £20 million plus.

The cost effectiveness of an aircraft with a life expectancy of perhaps half a dozen missions can only be justified against targets of exceptional importance or ones which 'smart' long-range missiles could not seek out as yet, such as mobile targets. The main battle tank (see Chapter 5) similarly is still the best asset in terms of mobile firepower on the land battlefield but two million dollar MBTs can be defeated by reliable, cheap wire-guided missiles and more significantly, at long range by the new generation of precision guided and advanced area weapons looked at later.

A very significant strand of military technological development therefore is towards the cheap and simple expendable platform carrying the sophisticated sensor or weapon system to the appropriate scene of action.

The 'remotely-piloted vehicle' (RPV) has a long history stretching back into the First World War but only in the late 1970s did 'drones' become a significant component of first division military forces while the success in 1982 of Israeli RPVs in the Lebanon in

This sequence shows the Copperhead laser-guided shell impacting on a tank target. There have been development problems particularly concerning the system's operability in weather conditions typical of northern European winters. The second problem is getting laser designators to the targets at Copperhead's maximum useful range. The Lockheed Aquila RPV presents one solution

reconnaissance and electronic intelligence missions has been eagerly analysed. The British Army has a number of Canadair 'Midge' USD-501 reconnaissance drones but these were not taken to the Falklands.

The US Army is bringing into operation an RPV system called Aquila. It looks like a miniaturised delta aircraft (which is just what it is) driven by a ducted pusher propeller with an airframe made of Kevlar. Aquila is launched from the back of a flatbed truck and is capable of undertaking missions of up to three hours at speeds up to 180 km/h, communicating in real time via a secure data link with its controllers. What is significant about Aquila is the payload — a tv camera or forward-looking infra-red (Flir), target tracker and laser designator/rangefinder in a stabilised mounting, all controlled by a microelectronic processor.

What Aquila sees is transmitted to the systems operations centre where mission commander, air vehicle operator and mission payload operator watch their monitors and control the mission. The mission payload operator controls the pointing and field of view of the tv camera and can actuate the ranging and target designation laser. With a target sighted, the co-ordinates can either be computed and transmitted to artillery batteries or

the laser designator will illuminate the target for laser seeking weapons such as laser-guided bombs (LGBs) looked at later. The operator can select an automatic tracking mode that keeps the stabilised camera and laser boresighted on the target regardless of the Aquila's movements, or it can be locked on to suspected targets that can be emphasised for the Aquila's own computer by the controller using a light pen on his display console.

The Aquila is typical of the relatively simple RPV systems now under development for taking the all-important seeing eyes of the new technology deep into hostile territory. Other RPVs are being developed to carry not just sensors but warheads which might be used to attack priority targets such as electronic warfare installations, radar and surface-to-air missile sites.

Laser-Guided Bombs

Laser-guided bombs (LGBs) were first devised in the mid-1960s at the height of the Viet Nam War where the first use of 'smart' bombs was made. The US Air Force's Paveway series has been considerably refined since then but the principle remains the same, an add-on seeker and control system which turns the free-fall bomb into a precision-guided munition.

The modification consists of a seeker in the extreme nose, in a pivoting housing controlled by an annular vane. Behind this comes a control section housing the computer, battery, control surface actuation mechanism and the control surfaces themselves.

This is how it works — the annular vane bomb needs no tracking or lock on before launch or any kind of electrical connection to the launch aircraft. When in range of the target, the bomb is released and flies ballistically towards it. The annular vane keeps the seeker head pointing towards the bomb's notional point of impact — wherever that should be, but within the seeker head is a four-quadrant photocell. Anything in its field of view which has been sparkled with laser energy will show up as a heat trace.

The seeker will filter out all but the infrared of any heat trace in its field of view and focus it onto the four-quadrant photocell. Any aiming errors will be interpreted as differences in the amount of energy falling on each quadrant, the guidance microprocessor interprets these differences and turns them into commands for the canard control surfaces to bring the system into balance with equal amounts of energy falling onto each quadrant. When this happens the seeker, and now the entire weapon, is heading straight for the source of energy.

That source will be target-illuminated by a laser designator — a remote laser mounted in an aircraft, on an RPV such as Aquila, or in the hands of an infantryman, and directed at a target to 'sparkle' it. The laser transmits coded pulses to which the seeker head is tuned so as not to home on the designator itself nor onto any other energy sources.

The laser-guided bomb represents a half-

DEEP STRIKE AND FOLLOW ON FORMATION ATTACK

NATO's problem in defending its Centre Sector from a theoretical Soviet attack is how to stop a massive and powerful enemy without resort to nuclear weapons in time for reinforcements to arrive. The US Army has recently adopted the doctrine of 'AirLand Battle' which puts emphasis on the power of the offensive and the so-called 'deep battle', that is engaging on the enemy's second and third wave both with actual manoeuvre forces on the ground and deep strike weapon systems. The NATO alliance also adopted in 1984 a variation of the idea which emphasises deep strike conventional firepower as a way of 'raising the nuclear threshold', rather than offensive manoeuvre operations and the 'integrated' use of nuclear weapons.

Both ideas hinge on the perception of the Soviet Army as attacking in echeloned waves, arrayed scores of kilometres behind the forward edge of the battle area. These mobile forces themselves (1) represent targets for new technology target acquisition and deep strike systems while attacks on fixed sites such as SAM sites and airfields (2) will determine the outcome of the air war, far more than one to one duels in the air. Attacks on the enemy Command and Control network by offensive electronic warfare systems (3) will further degrade his combat power. 'Interdiction' attacks on bridges and communications centres (4) will further delay the arrival of follow on forces at the front line.

way stage in the development of the precision-guided munition in that it needs a continuous laser illumination from an outside source and is not an all-weather system. The ambitious Copperhead laser-guided artillery shell programme for example has been plagued with development problems but is now in production for the US Army. In earlier trials it was shown that although it remained effective in dust and smoke, Copperhead would only work about half the time in the kind of conditions typical of a winter's day in Western Europe.

The next developmental thrust therefore is towards true 'fire-and-forget missiles' with their own autonomous target acquisition and discrimination systems using imaging infrared, millimetre-wave radar and/or other optical seekers. Such a system is a component of the US Air Force development programme called WAAM (Wide Area Anti-Armor Munitions) which includes advanced cluster munitions, scatterable mines and, the most ambitious of all, an autonomously homing anti-armour mini-missile called 'Wasp'.

Wasp is intended to give the launch aircraft almost complete freedom from the need to even see intended targets, let alone designate them. The aircraft becomes a simple carrier, a platform for smart weapons, merely hauling them towards the scene of action, and releasing them before getting into harm's way itself.

After launch, a swarm of Wasps will fly on

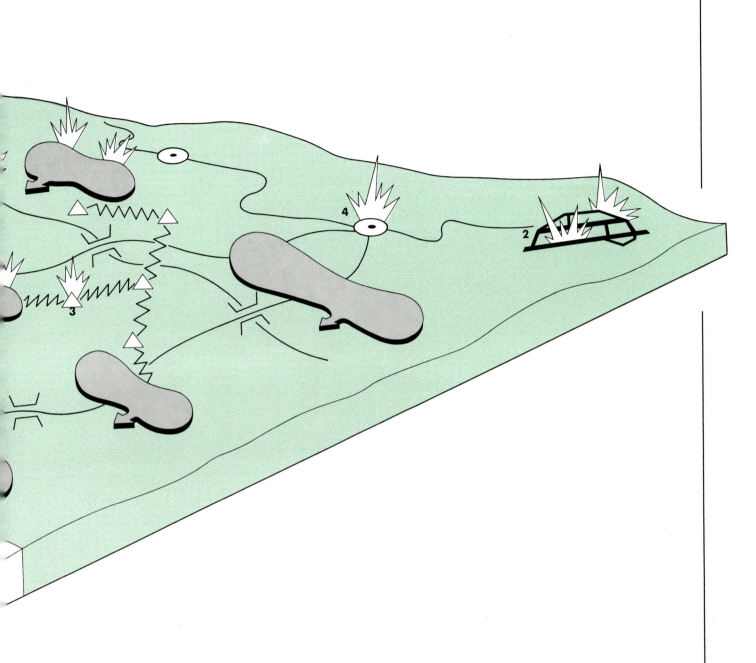

inertial guidance to the scene of action, the target co-ordinates acquired possibly by an RPV. The Wasp's own smart terminal guidance seeker now takes over, staring at the ground and picking up hot metallic targets, either through imaging infra-red or millimetric radar. Both function in the dark, at night or in battlefield smoke. The missile's own guidance computer will tell it whether the target is a tank or not and where to attack the target's weakest points — its thin top armour.

The US Air Force's WAAM programme is itself a component of the much wider Joint Armor Engagement System Study with US Army and Air Force projects funded and co-ordinated by the Defence Research Projects

Agency (DARPA). The US Army's technology development programme was called Assault Breaker with the objective of providing systems which could engage strong armoured formations well beyond the so-called Forward Edge of Battle Area (FEBA) or where the fighting forces actually met.

This goes back to the doctrine of forward defence with NATO strategists realising that new technology might be able to build in the depth that NATO sorely lacked — but it could be at the Warsaw Pact's expense by deploying deep strike weapons which could engage enemy 'follow on formations' up to 200 kilometres beyond the FEBA, and transform the battle from being a desperate attempt by NATO to hold the line into an invitation to an

*RAF Jaguar strike aircraft equipped with Paveway laser-guided bombs. LGBs allow close support strike missions to be delivered with a high degree of precision against targets illuminated by infantry in contact equipped with laser designators such as the Hughes Ground Laser Locator Designator (**inset**)*

aggressor to walk into a high technology trap that would invite the destruction of his entire forces — not just the first echelon, but the second and third, the theatre reserve and strategic reserve. Meanwhile long-ranging stand-off weapons would be attacking 'interdiction' targets such as roads and railways leading to the front line, airfields, control centres and so-on. The power of the precision-guided munition, it is argued, has given back to defence the deadly stopping power the machine gun had against infantry in 1914 before the dawn of the tank.

Some, while recognising the importance of the technological change, urge that priority be given now to stopping the irresistible force of the *first* echelon. If it means concentrating less on wonder weapons then so be it — what is needed is to stop the blitzkrieg cold by using every available existing weapon — ten Milan anti-tank missiles in the hand now are better than two smarter ones in ten years' time — so they argue. It cannot be denied that the cost of a weapon system rises exponentially with the depth of the target to be engaged.

Meanwhile NATO formally adopted Follow on Formation Attack (FOFA) as alliance policy in 1984 with weapon procurement programmes shaped to meet its requirements. The US Army adopted in 1982 a revised operational doctrine, incorporated in its standard field manual FM-100-5, called Air-Land Battle which expressed the totality of the combat environment emphasising manoeuvre and deep strike rather than static or backward rolling defence.

The strains this puts on command, control and communications (C^3) can be imagined. The new technologies expand distance and compress time. The process of acquiring and striking a target which today might take five hours, could with autonomous systems take a matter of minutes and once again only the microchip can handle the enormous load of data management this entails. The electronic battlefield therefore makes Electronic Warfare of every increasing importance.

One of the arguments against the philosophies of 'deep strike' and follow-on formation attack is that they will divert effort from systems at the critical front line where infantry armed with comparatively cheap but nevertheless sophisticated weapons can have considerable stopping power. The light infantry platoon armed with anti-tank missiles is still a formidable foe.

Right top: *Milan-armed infantry*

Right: *The M901 Improved TOW vehicle equips US Army mechanised infantry divisions*

Far right: *Sighting Milan from an IFV*

5 THE MAIN BATTLE TANK

Modern Tank Warfare

The tank, instrument of the German Blitzkrieg that took Europe by storm in 1940 and a symbol of oppression for today on city streets from Prague to Santiago, remains the principal arbiter of land warfare. The imbalance of armour between NATO and the Warsaw Pact provided the excuse for the deployment of tactical nuclear weapons in the first place, however the joint exercises of both alliances still centre on developing and repelling armoured thrusts by 'conventional' means. In real life wars meanwhile, tanks continue to slug it out on Third World battlefields.

The tank's importance in modern warfare is easy to explain. In any tactical situation fire and movement are the basic tools of attacker and defender alike, and the tank is able to deliver both. Infantry are needed to occupy territory, the basic aim of conventional warfare, but without tanks they are unlikely to find any to occupy, and the efforts of all other arms are dedicated to supporting the armoured spearhead that the tank represents. Advances in anti-tank weapons have been met by improvements in protection, and even in the face of tactical nuclear weapons, the tank crew is better placed to survive than most.

The tactics of armoured warfare have not changed fundamentally since the Second World War, and the basic concepts applied then, basically Blitzkrieg and infantry support, were themselves initially developed in the 1920s. The one emphasises movement, relying on rapid penetration of the enemy front line and the exploitation of the resulting disruption and dislocation of the opposing forces to achieve results; the other depends on more traditional concepts of positional warfare, subordinating movement to firepower.

At various stages the specific tactical requirements involved have resulted in the production of ranges of specialised tanks. Light, medium and heavy varieties, with progressively reduced mobility and increased firepower and protection, are exemplified by the light M41 Walker Bulldog, the medium M47 and M48 Patton and the heavy M103 bought by the US Army in the early 1950s; the Soviet Army similarly developed a series of heavy tanks culminating in the T-10 and the amphibious PT-76 light tank. However, since the early 1960s there has really only been one type, the medium or main battle tank (MBT), with other varieties of armoured vehicle being devoted to helping the infantry stay with it in the assault, or to providing more specialised support. There has also been one principal proving ground for both vehicles and tactics.

In 1967 Israel achieved a brilliant military success against Egypt, Syria and Jordan, largely on the strength of bold and decisive armoured operations, but in the early stages of the 1973 war against Egypt and Syria many tanks were lost to infantry anti-tank weapons as the Israeli advance on the Sinai front ground to a halt. This led to a widespread expression of opinion that the days of armoured supremacy were at an end, opinion which ignored the fact that it was the subsequent crossing of the Suez Canal and the armoured thrust into Egypt that restored the situation in Israel's favour. In fact the lessons to be drawn from the 1973 operations are more concerned with operational and organisational requirements: that tactical air superiority, effective artillery and infantry support and efficient co-ordination of all three are essential to successful armoured operations. Since 1973 the threat posed by the shaped-charge warheads of infantry anti-tank weapons has been countered by improved armour, while new threats have appeared, all of which have a bearing on the situation in Western Europe.

The Warsaw Pact has a substantial superiority of at least three to one in sheer tank numbers over its NATO opposition. The role of these in a projected conventional war in Europe, in conjunction with the rest of the formidable forces available, is to destroy a significant proportion of the opposing forces and occupy economically important areas as quickly as possible. Speed is important if NATO is to be forestalled in the use of theatre nuclear weapons; once the theatre has shifted behind NATO lines, their use would simply destroy the territory they are ostensibly there to defend, and the whole strategy is designed to achieve a result within the 'few days' for which the Western alliance is committed to refraining from going nuclear.

The basic operational formations are tank and motor rifle divisions, the former with ten tank and six motor rifle battalions, the latter with ten of motor rifle troops and seven of tanks. Respective strengths in tanks are 331 and 272. Within the divisions, individual battalions form regiments which may include predominantly tank or motor rifle components in a three-to-one ratio. At the basic level, tanks operate in companies of ten, mechanised infantry in companies of 12 vehicles; each combat regiment includes an artillery battalion with eighteen 122 mm self-propelled howitzers, while other supporting elements are organised at divisional level.

From battalion level up, combat teams and formations are organised as the tactical situation demands, and even divisions are subordinated to armies or fronts (the equivalent of

The Soviet T-72 is reported to have a high degree of protection across its frontal arc against the current generation of anti-tank guided weapons. It would however be vulnerable to top attack weapons

Western army groups). The result is a very powerful force, attacking with great organisational flexibility along the whole of a front: its objective is to breach the line of defence and penetrate far behind, relying on surprise and overwhelming strength for the initial breakthrough and exploiting it with maximum speed using division-size Operational Manoeuvre Groups (OMGs), possibly followed up by army-size OMGs. The former would be expected to advance at a rate of 100 kilometres (62 miles) a day, and would have as its objectives the destruction of nuclear weapons, C³ and air defences, disruption of lines of communication, occupation of airfields and the establishment of bridgeheads and secure routes for the main force. The higher level of OMG would be expected to press on through the disrupted defences three or four days after the initial breakthrough — scheduled for day 1 of the offensive — to seize key military and political objectives, including major urban and industrial centres.

In preparing to counter such an offensive NATO is hampered by the political need to form a forward line of defence and, in the light of Soviet strategy, this needs to be a continuous line. Moreover, even with constant satellite surveillance designed to give advance warning of a preliminary build-up, the Soviet emphasis on surprise is deliberately intended to minimise the time available for the long-range deployments the formation

The M1 Abrams is the US Army's latest main battle tank, powered by a gas turbine and protected by composite armour. In spite of its size and weight it has outstanding speed and agility on the battlefield with formidable firepower under the control of a ballistic computer which allows it to fire on the move

of this line would require. One means of countering the Soviet threat involves the use of sophisticated new weapons to destroy rear-echelon formations as part of the AirLand Battle 2000 scenario dealt with elsewhere; in the meantime, NATO policy is one of flexible response, the forward defence being backed up by the threat of theatre nuclear weapons.

The essence of forward defence is to use every available anti-tank weapon in a systematic attack on the advancing armoured formations, starting with heavy artillery at 20-kilometre ($12\frac{1}{2}$-mile) or more ranges and continuing down to shoulder-fired weapons at a few hundred metres, and using helicopters, fixed-wing aircraft and armoured vehicles to deploy rapidly in response to local needs. Available anti-tank weapon systems are examined later; in the meantime we should take a closer look at the object of all this attention.

Design and Technology
The modern main battle tank (MBT) represents the culmination of decades of development. The British Medium A Whippet of the First World War was the first tank recognisably to carry its guns on top and to be designed to move at cavalry rather than infantry pace; the German PzKpfw I of the late 1930s added a rotating turret, though mounting only a 20 mm gun and a 7·92 mm machine gun, a deficiency rectified by the 50 mm and 75 mm guns of the PzKpfw II and III. Meanwhile, the Soviet T-34/76, comparatively crude in construction but rugged and straightforward, cheap and simple to build and operate, well protected by thick, well-angled armour and carrying a powerful 76 mm gun, had the overwhelming advantage of availability in numbers great enough to swamp the German opposition. The T-34/76 also established a balance between the conflicting requirements of mobility, firepower and protection which directly inspired the German Panther, one of the cornerstones of subsequent Western tank development, and which has been maintained in a succession of Soviet tank designs whose evolution has continued into modern times.

The T-34/85 was the first step, a new 85 mm gun providing improved firepower, and by 1945 a developed version of the T-34/85 turret had been matched to a new, lower hull to form the T-44; this hull was enlarged to take the D-10T 100 mm gun in the T-54 of 1949; and by 1958 the D-10TS as used by the T-54B, an uprated engine and an improved suspension had been combined to produce the T-55. At this point there were major changes, when further modifications to

hull and suspension were accompanied by a new 115 mm U-5T smooth-bore gun with automatic loading and an integrated fire-control system in the shape of the T-62 of 1961.

A more powerful 125 mm version of the T-62's gun was mounted in a new hull to produce the T-64, in service by 1970 but little seen, and possibly something of an abortive offshoot from the mainstream of Soviet tank design. The T-64 has been restricted to Soviet service, but the subsequent T-72, using a similar hull and turret and the same gun along with an uprated engine, has been prominently displayed and widely exported, and is now being built in Yugoslavia. The latest Soviet MBT, the T-80, has continued the evolutionary process, combining an improved 125 mm gun in a turret with compound armour and a new engine in a T-64 hull. The compound armour on hull and turret have, however, resulted in a major escalation in weight: the T-72, at a combat weight of 41 tonnes, was less than ten per cent heavier than the T-62 of a decade earlier, but the T-80 weighs in at around 48 tonnes. Nevertheless, the improved armour was a necessity in a modern tank, and actually restores the balance with the increased firepower of the T-62 and the enhanced mobility provided by the T-72.

The current generation of Western MBTs also shows a move toward a balance between the three fundamental requirements, though with more or less pronounced national bias toward one or the other and with a rather more wayward development history. In doing so they have reflected partly the tactical preoccupations of the armies they were designed to serve and partly the technology available at various stages. There have been major advances in all three areas, each of which have necessarily had implications for the others.

New forms of projectile and, more recently, improvements in armour helped keep the tank in the game since the advent of hollow-charge anti-tank weapons, in the form of the American Bazooka in 1942, first appeared to threaten its extinction. Inexorable weight increases, even in Soviet tanks, have been more than matched by refinements in power trains. And even the various, often conflicting strands of Western tank design have begun to merge to the point where the latest American and German tanks, the M1 Abrams and Leopard 2, have become outwardly almost indistinguishable as well as remarkably similar internally.

Since the main enemy of the MBT remains another MBT, firepower and protection are inextricably linked. The first major postwar

The light tank still fulfills its traditional role of reconnaissance and is useful in lower intensity operations. This is a 30-mm cannon armed Scimitar of the British army, the crew in full NBC kit. Vehicles of this type were used operationally in the Falklands campaign

breakthrough was the armour-piercing discarding sabot (APDS) shot, a British development initially applied to anti-tank guns late in
World War II. With a 105 mm gun firing
APDS shot, late models of the Centurion —
itself a wartime product of a specification for
a 'universal' tank to replace the earlier
categories of 'infantry' and 'cruiser' types —
established it as the leading MBT of the 1950s
and 1960s, despite very poor mobility.

The discarding sabot has continued to be
used in newer types of kinetic energy anti-
tank projectiles — that is, those which rely on
the penetrative ability of a solid mass rather
than high-explosive energy. Since kinetic
energy is a function of the square of velocity
and the mass of the projectile, high velocities
are vital. The penetrators themselves are
made of tungsten or, more recently, depleted
uranium; the alloy sabot, or sleeve, enclosing
the penetrator in the gun barrel reduces
overall weight to less than that of a full-calibre
steel shot, helping to increase muzzle velocity
while concentrating the energy of the propellant charge in the high-density penetrator.

Further increases in muzzle velocities were
made possible by the adoption of smooth-
bore guns firing spin-stabilised projectiles. Fin
stabilisation also enabled the length-to-
weight ratio of the penetrator to be increased
beyond the 7:1 that is the practical limit for
fin-stabilised shells fired from rifled barrels,
to produce the current 'long-rod' type of
penetrators.

The Soviet Union introduced a smooth-
bore 125 mm gun on the T-62 in the early
1960s, and by the late 1970s the US Army had
decided to adopt the 120 mm smooth-bore
gun developed for the German Leopard 2.
While such weapons are marginally less accurate than rifled guns, and fire a comparatively
limited range of much more expensive projectiles, these are of greater mass and are
delivered at higher velocities to offer a better
single-shot kill probability. It is significant
that even the British, whose preference for
rifled guns is partly a consequence of their
greater versatility, are developing fin-stabilised long-rod projectiles which, with slipping
plastic driving bands, will be fired by a new
gun to be carried by the old Chieftain and the
new Challenger.

The other methods of attacking tanks,
using the chemical energy of high explosives,
involve focusing such energy in one of two
ways to achieve penetration of the armour.
High-explosive plastic (HEP) or squash-head
(HESH) shells have frangible nose cones
which break up on impact, explosive charges
which splatter against the surface of the
armour and base fuzes which then detonate
them; shock waves are transmitted through

the armour and reflected by the inner plate, causing stresses which result in scabs being detached from the inside and ricocheting around the inside of the vehicle.

The more effective high-explosive anti-tank (HEAT) shells have hollow nose cones and explosive charges formed with a convex cone. On detonation, again by base fuze, the cone focuses the gases produced into a fine jet, projected forward to burn through the armour and into the tank interior.

HEP/HESH has the inherent drawbacks that it can be prematurely detonated by spaced armour, its effectiveness can be degraded by surface obstacles interfering with the wave formation or by angled strikes causing the explosive to spread, and it requires a fairly hefty charge — 11 kilograms (25 pounds) or more — to achieve penetration. The effectiveness of hollow-charge shells, on the other hand, depends on the diameter of the charge and any HEAT shell of over 75 mm calibre is likely to defeat any practical conventional armour. Its lethality can be enhanced by using nose-cone liners which will form particles in the gas stream, or

The Soviet Army has long been a specialist in combat vehicles designed to provide organic short range air defence for ground forces on the move. The US Army has striven to catch up with the DIVAD (Divisional Air Defense) gun mounted on a tracked platform with twin radar controlled 40 mm cannon

by adding a resonator behind the charge, and spaced armour offers no protection. The performance of HEAT shells is, though, degraded by spinning. Smooth-bore guns were produced initially to fire fin-stabilised hollow-charge (HEATFS) ammunition, and its effects have been partly mitigated by interior redesign aimed at reducing fire risk. However, it was the introduction of compound armour that really confirmed the trend toward kinetic energy as the primary means of attacking tanks.

Current Western tank guns are of either

105 mm or 120 mm calibre, the former being derivatives of the British L7 rifled gun, built in the US as the M68 and used on the American M60 and M1, the German Leopard 1 and the Swedish S-tank; the latter are either rifled (the British L11 on Chieftain and Challenger) or smooth-bore (the Rheinmetall gun carried by Leopard 2 and future variants of M1). As outlined earlier, Soviet tanks have mounted smooth-bore guns for some years, with the 115 mm weapons carried by the T-62 and T-64 giving way to a 125 mm weapon for the T-72 and T-80. Ammunition stowage ranges from the 40 rounds of the T-62 to 64 rounds in the Chieftain; Challenger reduces this total to 50, while the T-80 and M1 accommodate 55 and Leopard 1 and 2 have 60.

Performance of a tank gun can only be as good as the mounting and fire-control systems by which it is laid. Powered turrets with automatic gun stabilisation to keep the gun pointing at the target while the tank is on the move have been standard for some years, but recent advances in micro-electronics have had an almost revolutionary impact on the speed and accuracy of gun-laying. Early fire-control systems slaved the gun to an optical sight which the gunner lined up with the target, stadiametric or coincidence type optical rangefinders were used to determine target range, and a mechanical computer calculated gun elevation based on the range data. Ranging was improved by the introduction of coaxial ranging machine guns, pioneered by the Centurion in the early 1950s, but as effective gun ranges increased beyond 2000 metres (6560 feet) they outstripped that of the ranging MG, and the real breakthrough was the introduction of laser rangefinders with an accuracy of ±5 metres (16·4 feet). Coupled with ballistic computers these enable both accurate and, equally important, rapid firing solutions to be achieved, improving hit probability and reducing engagement times.

The gunner's main sight in a modern MBT is stabilised at least in elevation, and the main gun and coaxial machine gun are slaved to it. The computer stores data on the performance of different types of ammunition, and variations between different batches of the same type, and sensors provide it with information on factors which will affect the ballistic solution, such as wind speed and direction, ambient temperature and the temperature of the propellant, barometric pressure, barrel wear and temperature, angle of sight and the displacement of the line-of-sight from the gun bore axis; these may be entered automatically or manually by the gunner. In order to reduce aiming errors thermal jackets are used to maintain the gun barrel at a uniform

ANTI-TANK MISSILE GUIDANCE

Missile guidance for anti-tank missiles has progressed through two generations with the third 'fire and forget' generation beginning to appear. Wire-guided manual command to line of sight systems (MCLOS) such as the BAe Swingfire require considerable skill of the operator who has to keep both target and missile in his line of sight. An MCLOS missile flies slowly with a flight time of up to 20 secs. The second generation Semi Automatic to Line of Sight (SACLOS) requires the operator to track the target only with an automatic guidance package tracking a flare on the missile doing the rest

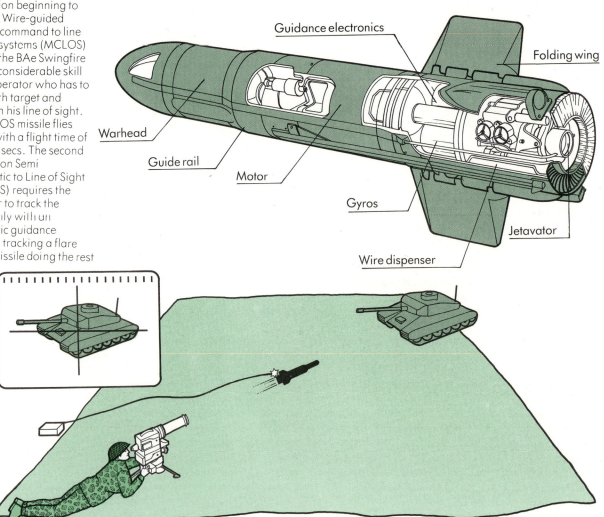

Guidance electronics

Folding wing

Warhead

Guide rail

Motor

Gyros

Jetavator

Wire dispenser

temperature so that barrel droop can be calculated accurately, and allowance is made for gun jump as the projectile exits from the muzzle.

The gunner's sight itself will normally have adjustable magnification and field of view, either a single or a binocular eyepiece, a thermal imaging system for use in darkness or bad weather, and a laser rangefinder. On identifying the target, the gunner aligns the sight and activates the rangefinder, selects and enters ammunition type on his control panel, and the computer will either lay the gun automatically on command or provide a computed aiming point in the eyepiece which the gunner lays over the target; when it is ready to fire another visual cue is provided in the eyepiece. The tank commander has his own sight, either duplicating the gunner's view or using an independent system to enable him to scan for fresh targets during an engagement, and he is able to control the firing sequence by overriding the gunner's controls.

Such sophistication enables targets to be acquired and engaged in only a few seconds, with first-round hit probabilities of the order of 80 per cent against stationary targets at ranges of up to 3000 metres (9850 feet) and moving targets at up to 2000 metres (6560 feet), assuming standard NATO tank turret targets of 2·3 square metres (25 square feet).

Another important factor affecting survivability is the degree of armour protection provided. With only a small additional weight penalty this all-round protection can be increased to the point where it will withstand larger-calibre machine gun rounds, small calibre cannon shells and high-explosive artillery shells. To protect against specialised anti-tank weapons, however, ten or more times the basic armour thickness is needed, involving considerable additional weight.

The widespread use of guided missiles and infantry anti-tank weapons with shaped-charge warheads led to the development of compound armour. Essentially, compound armour involves an arrangement of layers or plates of various materials with spaces between. The spaces help render HEP/HESH charges ineffective, while the nature and arrangement of the plates combine to absorb the energy of kinetic energy penetrators and the hot gases of HEAT shell charges. At the same time, it is heavy and bulky — it is responsible for an increase of almost 20 per cent in the weight of the latest Soviet design compared with its immediate predecessor. It therefore cannot be applied all round in place of conventional armour but is used in the form of add-on packs to protect the most exposed areas.

Other forms of add-on armour include ceramic tiles, which can be positioned around the turret and hull front, and the still newer 'active armour', which uses a thin layer of explosive, detonated on the impact of an incoming round, to disrupt the action of a shaped-charge warhead.

In action a tank will naturally expose its turret more than its hull, even if it is dug into a firing position it must expose its turret to fire, and on the move terrain features will shield the hull before the turret. The turret is therefore the most heavily armoured part of the tank. Its front and sides are thickly armoured and sloped or curved to deflect kinetic energy or HEP/HESH rounds. Compound armour has had an effect on turret design: tanks designed to wear compound armour such as Challenger, Leopard 2 and M1 Abrams have slab-sided turrets. The other area given heavy armour is the upper hull front.

Typical maximum armour thicknesses are likely to be of the order of 120 to 200 mm (4·75 to 8·87 inches); exact figures are rarely revealed, but of the last generation of Western tanks Chieftain was acknowledged to be the most heavily armoured. The American M60's maximum thickness was 120 mm (4·75 inches) and Germany's Leopard 1, designed with the emphasis on mobility, was very lightly armoured; respective weights for the three tanks are 55, 49 and 39·5 tonnes. The contemporary Soviet T-62, with a weight of only 37·5 tonnes, was also lightly armoured, relying for protection on its rounded turret and low silhouette; the T-72, with a published weight of 41 tonnes, is unofficially reported to have 200 mm (7·87 inches) of steel frontal armour or, in another version, 100 mm (3·94 inches) each of steel and compound armour. The current generation of tanks is appreciably heavier, with Challenger, M1 Abrams and Leopard 2 weighing in at 61, 54·5 and 55 tonnes respectively, while even the Soviet T-80, as noted earlier, is estimated to weigh 48·5 tonnes. All these figures reflect the addition of compound armour.

Internal fire suppression is important, since HEAT shells rely on the secondary effects of the hot gas stream for much of their lethality. In this context, the switch from petrol to diesel fuel in self-sealing tanks has proved helpful; additional measures include carrying the propellant charges separately in individual compartments whose double walls are filled with pressurised water and glycol or other fire-extinguishing fluid; providing blow-off doors to release blast.

A further threat which must be considered is the use of NBC (nuclear, chemical or biological) weapons. NBC protection has

INFANTRY WEAPONS

How can it be in the age of automated warfare and precision guided munitions that flesh and blood infantrymen should have a place on the battlefield? They do so because it is still the man on the ground who can achieve the objectives of war, not just the seizing of an objective but its holding. Airmen or submariners cannot hold ground or take a surrender. Mechanised forces cannot fight across the spectrum of warfare from guerilla operations via jungle warfare up to the high intensity integrated battlefield that operations on NATO's central front would entail. As the US Army's field manual outlines the role of infantry —

'to occupy strongpoints as pivots for maneuver; to make initial penetrations for exploitation by armor and mechanised infantry;
to attack over approaches that are not feasible for heavy forces;
capture or defend built up areas; control restrictive routes for use by other forces; follow and support exploiting heavy forces.

In the Falklands fighting it was British infantry who secured the strategic objectives of an Argentinian surrender once air and sea power had brought them in range of their objective and they did so manoeuvring by epic forced marches with armoured forces operating only in the margins. But they did have the assistance of high technology, whether expressed in waterproof combat clothing or in the night observation devices (NOD) that allowed operations to continue in conditions that baffled the enemy.

Technology is a two-edged sword. While it concentrates intensely lethal firepower in a modern artillery system for example it also devolves giant-slaying stopping power on the individual soldier. In the Middle East war of 1973 wire-guided, infantry-portable anti-tank missiles at last gave the single, well-trained soldier the ability to match the armoured fighting vehicle. Defensive AFV technology to some extent has caught up but so has the mechanised infantryman who now rides to battle in the kind of specialised infantry fighting vehicles such as the US Bradley and Soviet BMP discussed on page 108 from which the infantry squad can either fight mounted or dismounted armed with third generation precision-guided anti-tank missiles. Fighting in either way moreover, infantrymen can use such devices as laser designators and sophisticated electronic systems to call up devastating and precise firepower.

Meanwhile the 'traditional' weapons of the infantry have themselves been subject to the high technology revolution from personal weapons such as assault rifles and sub-machine guns, via night observation devices and thermal imagers to the infantry's own portable artillery — mortars.

Left: *British infantryman armed with the US manufactured AR-15 assault rifle. The weapon fires a 5·56 mm bullet at a velocity of 1000 metres per second. It has a twenty-round magazine with a cyclic rate of fire of 700 rounds per minute*

Right: *Flesh and blood infantrymen are becoming the platforms themselves for sophisticated sensors such as the Pilkington Nova passive night vision monocular shown here. Night capable target acquisition and observation devices could revolutionise the pace of land warfare*

Below: *Airborne and airmobile forces have special problems in fighting without heavy weapons. This is the French Lohr L500 lightweight 4 × 4 vehicle equipped with Milan designed for use by airborne troops*

The British Army's Challenger main battle tank features the massive slab sided appearance associated with composite armour. Main armament is a 120 mm gun firing an advanced fin-stabilised round

become standard, and consists primarily of air filtration systems to provide uncontaminated air at a pressure high enough to keep the outside air from entering an open hatch or leaking through defective seals. The crew would still need to wear NBC protective clothing to guard against malfunction of the air-conditioning equipment, which is often carried in the turret bustle, or holing of the pressurised compartment. In the case of nuclear weapons, both conventional and compound armour already provide an effective measure of protection against alpha, beta and gamma radiation, but do little to inhibit neutrons, though it has been claimed that a feasible boron lining could reduce vulnerability to neutron radiation from a conventional low-yield nuclear weapon.

Despite all these measures, and even assuming that no penetration of the armour takes place, the force of a hit by a kinetic energy projectile is likely to at least stun the crew and may well disable the tank through systems or structural damage. Crew survival is regarded as particularly important by Western armies, and damage limitation is important if the tank is to be repaired and returned to action, but in the immediate context of the battle the indirect protection afforded by minimising the chance of being hit assumes equal importance.

Hit avoidance is largely a function of mobility. A tank may be relatively safe from detection while concealed and camouflaged in a defensive position, but it must expose its gun to fire, increasing the risk of detection, and once it has fired it has almost certainly revealed its position. Since modern fire-control systems have reduced gun-laying and firing times to a few seconds, any further reduction in the period of exposure to counter-fire can only be achieved by reducing the time taken to return to cover after firing. Similarly, an attacking tank on the move will seek to move rapidly between covered firing positions, and keeping the intervals of exposure to a minimum translates directly into speed and acceleration.

Agility — the ability to turn in a small radius and surmount obstacles and cross gaps in uneven terrain — is another important factor both in enabling defending tanks to make use of any available firing position and allowing an attacker to make maximum use of available cover. Reliability and fuel consumption have a bearing on the ability of a tank to travel long distances under its own power and to go directly into action.

Tanks are equipped to create their own temporary cover in the form of smoke, produced either by grenades fired from turret-mounted smoke dipensers or, as is common

in Soviet tanks, by burning fuel in the engine. Thermal imagers made smoke ineffective as far as opposing tanks are concerned, though infantry or vehicles without thermal imaging equipment would lose contact. However, thermal imagers are already being countered by new types of smoke generator which can produce smoke to block the infra-red wavelengths used by these systems, and whose air-bursting submunitions produce a nearly instantaneous smoke cloud. It is also possible to equip tanks with rocket-launchers whose chaff or pyrotechnic payloads will act as decoys for radar or infra-red missiles.

However, mobility remains the key to minimising exposure times, and the fundamental factor involved is power-to-weight ratio. In the early 1960s, when the output of tank engines was restricted to around 560 kW (750 hp), the Chieftain and M60 had power-to-weight ratios of 10 kW/tonne (13·7 hp/ton) and 11·4 kW/tonne (15·3 hp/ton) respectively; the contemporary T-62, with only 433 kW (580 hp) available, had a ratio of 10·8 kW/tonne (14·5 hp/ton); while by 1965, with an engine developing 619 kW (830 hp) and weight kept to a minimum, the Leopard 1 was in service with a ratio of 15·5 kW/tonne (20·75 hp/ton) and a reputation for outstanding cross-country performance.

The current generation of tank engines offer much greater power — 895 kW (1200 hp) and 1119 kW (1500 hp) respectively for the 12-cylinder diesels powering Challenger and Leopard 2, and 1119 kW (1500 hp) for the M1 Abrams' gas turbine. So although vehicle weights have increased considerably, power-to-weight ratios have also improved markedly, to 20·3 kW/tonne (27·3 hp/ton) for Leopard 2, 21 kW/tonne (28·1 hp/ton) for M1 Abrams and 14·7 kW/tonne (19·7 hp/ton) for the 61-tonne Challenger, a figure approaching that for the 40-tonne Leopard 1 of less than two decades earlier.

These increased power levels and higher power-to-weight ratios have resulted in only modest increases in maximum road speeds — from 48 km/h (30 mph) for Chieftain and M60 to 56 km/h (35 mph) and 72 km/h (45 mph) for Challenger and M1 and from 65 km/h (40 mph) to 72 km/h (45 mph) for Leopard 1 and 2, the transmission instead being optimised for acceleration and turning performance. The latter is affected by the length of track on the ground and the distance between the two tracks: the longer the tracks, the further apart they need to be. At the same time, width restrictions imposed by considerations of size (and hence weight, cost and target area) and the need to use existing

The Bundeswehr's Leopard II is one of the most formidable of third generation main battle tanks. Like the Challenger and the M1 Abrams however, they may be the end of the evolutionary line

roads and bridges both in peacetime and during preliminary deployment, result in a conflict with the requirement to reduce ground pressure, which means increasing track area, for soft-ground operation.

In basic figures, all modern tanks can cross trenches of around 3 metres (9 feet 10 inches) and surmount vertical obstacles of 0·9 to 1·24 metres (3 feet to 4 feet 1 inch), as well as cope with gradients of up to 60 per cent. As far as wider water obstacles are concerned, a fording depth of one metre (3 feet 3·37 inches) presents few problems provided the bottom is reasonably firm and stable, and it is possible to equip tanks with seals and snorkels to enable them to cross deeper water courses submerged. The latter is a time-consuming procedure, however, and requires detailed reconnaissance and security of both banks. Specialised bridge-laying vehicles can lay bridges capable of supporting tanks across gaps of 20 metres (65 feet 6 inches) or so within about 15 minutes — particularly useful in Western Europe where such gaps are likely to be encountered at least every 25 kilometres (15½ miles). Wider obstacles, which occur proportionately less frequently, are still numerous and require more complicated solutions, usually in the form of a floating bridge assembled in sections.

Given the choices and frequent design conflicts outlined above, it is clear that the final form of a tank will depend on a series of compromises between the fundamental requirements of firepower, protection and mobility. In the first, highly developed tank guns are standard, and their associated fire-control systems have reached an advanced stage of development; it is doubtful whether guns will often be used at ranges greater than those over which a high first-round hit probability exists. Protection has been improved to deal better with shaped charges, the universal anti-tank missile warhead, and new techniques will be needed if missiles are to continue to be a major threat; but it is still limited, and even without penetration a short- or medium-range hit from another tank's high-velocity kinetic energy penetrator is likely to prove disabling. Mobility, meanwhile, has continued to improve despite hefty weight increases. The final choice concerns the precise proportions in which these are combined.

Broadly, of the previous generation, the British Chieftain was built to be able to outshoot its opponents, survive better and go anywhere on the battlefield, but slowly; the German Leopard 1 was designed to travel far and fast with a useful gun but limited protection; and the American M60, designed against a background of world-wide commitments on the part of the US Army and potential battlefields involving an extreme range of climatic conditions and a wide range of threats, was necessarily fairly well balanced.

The current generation of NATO MBTs show a much closer convergence: better mobility for the British Challenger, improved protection and a bigger gun for the Leopard 2, more of everything in similar proportions for the M1 Abrams. Soviet tank design has always concentrated on balance, and has achieved good results with vehicles of markedly smaller size than their Western contemporaries.

The characteristics of Soviet tanks which have enabled them to mount guns of equal or greater size and carry armour of comparable thickness to those of their NATO counterparts at such reduced weights are those which combine to reduce overall size. Transverse engine mountings and compact transmissions, as used until the T-62, had a significant effect in reducing volume; subsequent designs keep volume low by carrying less ammunition, carrying as much as half their basic fuel load externally, and providing less space for each member of a crew of three, an auto-loader replacing one of the four crew required by Western tanks; in addition, Soviet tank guns can only be depressed to about four degrees, compared with an average of ten degrees elsewhere. Again, these solutions reflect compromises which are regarded as acceptable in terms of Soviet resources and tactics: in the first place, they have more tanks, which would be expected to remain in the front line for shorter periods, so that ammunition requirements are less critical; the reduced crew space is accounted for by the simple expedient of restricting crew height to a maximum of 1·6 metres (5 feet 4 inches), presumably not a problem given the number of conscripts from which the Soviet Army can choose; and restricting gun depression angles is only a drawback in firing at negative angles, which would normally be the preserve of a defending tank moving up to a crest to fire at an attacker below; otherwise, restricted depression angles help reduce turret height, which is of greater help to a moving attacker, the more likely role for a Soviet machine.

Outside NATO and the Warsaw Pact, there are some interesting variations to meet specific tactical situations. The Swedish Stridsvagn 103, or S-tank, dispenses with a turret altogether in favour of a fixed gun laid by aligning the tank and adjusting its suspension to the required elevation. It is extremely well protected in terms of both substantial armour and reduced target area, and has good mobility with a combination of primary

Inside the turret of the French AMX-32 showing the commander's control panel. The integrated COTAC fire-control system with a laser rangefinder, ballistic computer and night optical sights allows the commander to designate targets and aim and fire the main armament even when the vehicle is moving

diesel engine and a gas turbine for additional power in cross-country operation. Highly innovatory, it suffers from some tactical drawbacks, principally an inability to fire on the move, but it has excellent defensive qualities and is the only unconventional design to have made a lasting impression.

The Israeli Merkava is more conventional in appearance, but is unique in mounting the engine and transmission in the front rather than the back of the hull for better crew protection, reflecting the special circumstance of Israel's very limited population. Along with a low, well-sloped turret goes a standard 105 mm rifled gun: this is smaller than those now in use elsewhere, but Israeli gunnery is

acknowledged as being the best in the world, and the new APFSDS projectile used has demonstrated an ability to penetrate the frontal armour of Syrian T-72s. Power-to-weight ratio is low at 12 kW/tonne (16 hp/ton), and road speed is consequently restricted to only 46 km/h (29 mph). However, the potential area of operations is also limited, and one consequence of the power train layout is the creation of an armoured compartment in the rear of the hull where extra ammunition or six equipped infantry can be carried.

Inside the Modern MBT

The latest generation of Western MBTs is represented by the American M1 Abrams and

INFANTRY COMBAT VEHICLES

Tanks, however sophisticated, cannot fight on their own. They need thorough reconnaissance before they can advance and infantry support during the advance. They also need specialised artillery, anti-aircraft and anti-tank weapons, as well as a multitude of back-up vehicles and resources.

The range of equipment and services required is illustrated by the composition of a US Army Heavy Division. This consists of five tank and five mechanised infantry battalions, allocated in variable proportions to three brigades and formed into battalion-size combined task forces by the brigade commander. The tank battalions comprise four companies of three platoons, each of which has four tanks, with scout, mortar and maintenance facilities provided at battalion level. The mechanised infantry battalion has four rifle companies with 13 infantry fighting vehicles distributed among three platoons, and an anti-tank company with 12 TOW-armed armoured personnel carriers (APCs). Direct support is provided by a self-propelled artillery brigade, with a 155 mm self-propelled howitzer battalion, another battalion of 8-inch self-propelled howitzers or the new Multiple Launch Rocket System vehicles, plus a target acquisition battery. There is also a Cavalry Brigade, Air Attack, comprising a Cavalry Squadron, with 40 Cavalry Fighting Vehicles, eight AH-64 attack helicopters and 12 OH-58 scout helicopters; two anti-tank helicopter battalions, each with 21 AH-64s, 13 OH-58s and three UH-60 assault transport helicopters; and a combat support battalion with 30 helicopters of various types.

Along with the five fighting brigades, there is a Divisional Support Command including maintenance, transport and three forward support battalions, while the headquarters formation provides signals, mechanical engineering and intelligence battalions plus military police and NBC companies. Ten of the US Army's 16 active combat divisions are heavy.

The vehicle that will be alongside the tanks in the front line of attack or defence is the MICV (mechanised infantry combat vehicle). This is a much more formidable vehicle than the old APC, from which it is distinguished by the fact that it carries its own tactical weapon system rather than just a defensive machine gun or two, and allows troops to fight from inside if necessary.

Current MICVs include the American M2 Bradley, German Marder, British MCV80 and Soviet BMP. Each carries a section of six to eight infantry, at least some of whom, except in MCV80, have firing ports so that they can use their assault rifles from inside the vehicle. All have an automatic turreted gun — 25 mm Chain Gun (Bradley), 20 mm cannon (Marder), 30 mm cannon (MCV80) or 73 mm smooth-bore low-pressure gun (BMP), the last replaced by a 30 mm cannon on the latest variant. The Bradley and BMP also carry launchers for wire-guided anti-tank missiles — two TOW with five reloads and one AT-6 Sagger respectively, the latter replaced by AT-5 Spandrel on new BMPs. The main guns fire both armour-piercing and high-explosive rounds for use against other light AFVs and soft targets, and a coaxial 7·62 mm machine gun is also carried.

MICVs are fully tracked to enable them to go wherever the tanks go, and are faster, to enable them to manoeuvre effectively and to deploy ahead of the tanks if necessary. Typically, the Soviet BMP is smaller, lighter, less well armoured and less powerful than its Western counterparts, and is in service in far greater numbers: compared with its 13·9-tonne combat weight and 224 kW (300 hp) engine, the 22·7-tonne Bradley has a 377 kW (506 hp) engine; respective maximum road speeds are 80 km/h (50 mph) and 66 km/h (41 mph).

Crew protection comes in the form of armour plate, though considerably lighter than that of an MBT, with aluminium alloys replacing steel for the structural shell, and NBC air-conditioning systems. The inadequate protection of the BMP has been highlighted in Afghanistan, where additional armour has had to be installed to protect the occupants from 12·7 mm machine gun fire.

MICVs also form the basis for specialised vehicles, with the BMP, the oldest and most numerous, having spawned the greatest number. Normally one of the MICVs in a platoon will have extra radio equipment for the platoon commander, while in the case of BMP there are also company and battalion command variants; reconnaissance versions, some with radar for use by divisional reconnaissance battalions or to carry out surveillance and targeting for artillery battalions; and small numbers adapted to carry mortars and to act as light recovery vehicles. The M3 Cavalry Fighting Vehicle variant of the M2 carries only two people in addition to the operating crew of three, and acts more as a light tank, with extra ammunition compared with the infantry model.

The latest of the MICVs to enter service, the British MCV80, was designed with a basic requirement to accommodate ten fully-equipped infantry and to sustain them for 48 hours on the battlefield. Mobility and protection were equal second in importance, and firepower last,

Right: *The pioneer infantry fighting vehicle able to carry a squad of infantry into the heart of battle and be armed with a system which could take on tanks was the Soviet BMP. The Germans introduced the comparable Marder (**below**) in the early '70s but the British and US armies are only just catching up with the deployment of the M2 Bradley and MCV 80*

with missiles rejected as a distraction from the vehicle's primary role.

The personnel compartment in the rear holds seven infantry and their equipment; access is via rear double doors and, with equipment stowed along the inside of the walls, there are no firing ports though there are periscopes to allow surveillance. The commander and gunner are accommodated in the turret and the driver in the left front of the hull. The turret is offset to the left of the vehicle to balance the weight of the 410 kW (550 hp) eight-cylinder diesel engine and automatic transmission in the right hull front. Maximum road speed is 75 km/h (47 mph) forward and 48 km/h (30 mph) in reverse.

the German Leopard 2. They are remarkable for their similarity in appearance and overall dimensions, though until 1970 the two countries were working on a joint design designated MBT70 so some technological resemblance was to be expected. Basic armament, powerplant and armour characteristics have already been described, but these are only part of the story: a tank is designed to be fought, and the crew environment is a major factor in determining combat efficiency.

Both tanks have a conventional crew arrangement, with the driver seated in the front of the hull. The principal control is a T-bar in M1, a curved yoke in Leopard 2, both of which are adjustable as is the Leopard 2's accelerator pedal; the M1 mounts the throttles on the T-bar hand grips. Automatic transmissions mean that the driver has only to select one of the four forward and two reverse gears in either case, and both vehicles provide three periscopes for use when the hatch is closed for action. Torsion bar suspension and seven road wheels are common to both, but while the Leopard 2's tracks need to be tensioned manually the M1 has a hydraulic tensioning system.

In the fighting compartment the positions are again conventional, with the gunner seated at a lower level than the commander on the right of the turret with the gun muzzle to his left, with the primary sight and control panel in front. The gunner also has a direct-view periscope in Leopard 2, while the commander in both vehicles has six periscopes for all-round vision. The Leopard 2 commander has his own rotating periscope which enables him to acquire targets and automatically hand them over to the gunner on the completion of the previous engagement, whereas in M1 the commander has only a take-off from the gunner's primary sight.

The loader sits on the left of the turret, while ammunition is stowed both in the hull and the turret bustle. The M1 stows 44 rounds in the bustle, with the remaining 11 distributed behind the commander and below the gun; only 15 rounds are stowed in Leopard 2's bustle, with the other 27 in the left front of the hull. Both tanks have a coaxial 7·62 mm machine gun, and Leopard 2 has another on a ring mounting round the loader's hatch; a similar arrangement on the M1 is supplemented by a 12·7 mm machine gun above the commander's station. The loader is also responsible for operating the radios, located in front of the loader's station in M1 but behind the commander in the German vehicle. Both loaders have access to the ready rounds in the bustle via button-operated automatic doors, and the Leopard 2's loader also has a hatch in the turret side for reple-

nishment of ammunition during battle. The Leopard 2 loader's periscope is fixed, while in M1 it rotates to enable the loader to help search for targets. Both main guns fire HEAT and APFSDS ammunition, but that for the 120 mm smooth-bore gun on Leopard 2 uses semi-combustible ammunition with a stub case to reduce the amount of waste metal accumulated during firing.

Both tanks incorporate a number of measures designed to enhance crew survivability. Fuel compartments and fuel and hydraulic lines are separated from the crew compartment, and fire detection and suppression systems are installed. A pressurised NBC air filtration system enables the Leopard crew to dispense with protective suits, while the M1 has the converse arrangement, US Army doctrine being to practise the wearing of NBC suits as routine on the grounds that the need to wear them in the event of the vehicle system failing would lead to impaired efficiency through lack of familiarity.

The detail differences between the two tanks may be less striking than the obvious similarities, but they do help to illustrate the amount of detail design involved in a weapon system as complex as an MBT. Many of the choices, such as the question of NBC protection, may be a matter of preference on the part of each service, but other elements, such as the lack of an independent sighting system for the M1 commander, reflect cost constraints, and only experience can show whether the ultimate choice was the right one.

Future MBTs
M1, Leopard 2 and Challenger may well prove to be the last tanks of their type. By the mid-1990s a new generation of MBTs will be

required to replace them, and military planners and industrial design teams are already at work. The next generation of armoured fighting vehicles (AFVs) is still at the concept formulation stage, but in recent years a number of more or less radical proposals have been made. Generally these are aimed at reducing size and weight, both as a contribution to survivability and as a means of reducing unit cost. Affordability has come to be a prime consideration in the design of modern weapon systems; budgets are limited, and it is an inescapable fact that sheer numbers are bound to have an influence on the outcome of an armoured battle. More-

over, reductions in size will also produce reductions in logistic support requirements, which vary roughly in accordance with the cube of tank weight.

It is unlikely that main armament will be anything but a high-pressure gun, possibly using liquid propellant for higher muzzle velocities, able to defeat both opposing MBTs and anti-tank helicopters, and for any worthwhile reduction in size an automatic loading system will have to be used. There are unlikely to be any alternatives to diesel or gas turbine in the way of powerplants, but these will have to be developed to give still greater power while avoiding large increases in

Far left: The British Army has a very large requirement for the MCV 80 infantry fighting vehicle, field trials of which began with the British Army of the Rhine in 1984. The chassis will form the basis of a range of specialised combat vehicles

Below: *The Bradley M2 IFV is armed with a 25 mm cannon and TOW anti-tank missiles*

ARTILLERY AND MINES

The military expression 'artillery' today covers guns, both towed and mounted on self-propelled platforms and surface-to-surface missiles. Tube and missile artillery can be used to deliver nuclear, chemical or conventional high explosives plus sub-munitions ranging from anti-armour weapons, mines or even electronic sensors. Tube artillery can bring down far greater intensity of firepower than missiles at the expense of range but weapons such as multiple rocket launchers and rocket assisted artillery projectiles are blurring the distinction.

Artillery has always meant warfare by numbers and computers have transformed the speed and accuracy of ballistic computation. Parallel advances in target acquisition and ammunition have made tube artillery a contender in the precision deep strike arena out to ranges of 30 km at least, as well as giving direct fire support at the front line.

The technology of tube artillery has developed along four lines — increasing the range by advances in ordnance and ammunition, increases in lethality by applying precision terminal guidance to artillery shells which may incorporate submunitions, increasing co-ordinated firepower by computerised fire control and communications and increasing tactical flexibility by emphasising self propelled mountings.

Cargo carrying artillery shells have been developed in tandem able to engage enemy forces directly by dispensing smart submunitions or by creating mined areas.

Tube artillery launched mines came under another umbrella US Army programme called FASCAM (Family of Scatterable Mines) which also embraces helicopter and fixed wing aircraft sowed systems and a ground based system called GEMSS which sows anti-armour or anti-personnel mines from a trailer towed behind wheeled or tracked vehicles, punching them out at preset 30 m intervals. The ability to lay down mine barriers quickly and at stand off range if necessary is regarded as being of great tactical significance for bringing new pace to the battlefield both in attack and defence.

Below: *The US M107 175 mm gun is in NATO-wide service. Those in US service have been converted to M110A1 standard capable of firing nuclear rounds. Maximum range with rocket-assisted projectiles is 30 km*

Right: *Heavy lift helicopters provide new mobility for towed artillery. Here a US Army Chinook lifts an M198 155'mm howitzer*

Below right: *The British Bar Mine system can lay up to 700 plastic anti-tank mines per hour. Normal tow vehicle is the FV432 armoured personnel carrier*

weight or volume. Protection will probably have to be modified to take account of top attack weapons, with more armour on the turret roof. On the other hand, some lines of research envisage the elimination of tank turrets.

In Sweden, a range of AFVs have been designed including such innovations as articulated chassis and externally-mounted guns which, unlike that of the S-tank, can be raised for traverse and elevation. To overcome the restrictions this would impose on all-round vision, it is possible to elevate the commander's cupola when the gun is in the firing position to enable him to see over it. An American design, the experimental HSTV-L (High Survivability Test Vehicle-Lightweight), has a very low profile turret with a 75 mm cannon mounted on forward trunnions and only the commander in the turret. However, such forward mountings mean that there is long barrel overhang, and a full-size tank gun would impose enormous strain on such a mounting.

The realignment of crew tasks, making full use of advanced technology, is another possibility. In a two-person turret, with commander and gunner on either side of the gun, the full duplication of all-round surveillance facilities would enable both to search for and either to engage a target while the other continued to watch for fresh targets or threats. At the same time, 'drive by wire' engine, gearbox and steering controls might enable the tank to be driven from the turret, either for hatch down manoeuvring and for reversing when the driver has to rely on instructions from the turret, or as a means of eliminating the driver altogether. Alternatively, the provision of television cameras and visual display units could enable the tank to be driven from the back of the hull as well as from the turret.

USAF armourers load Maverick missiles on an A-10 anti-tank aircraft
Below: *The US Chapparal air defence system is based on an adaptation of the Sidewinder heat-seeking air-to-air missile*

Anti-tank Weapons

The range of weapons deployed or under development by NATO for use against Warsaw Pact tanks is both varied and formidable. Discounting those intended for attacking rear-echelon formations, the onslaught is designed to start when the leading attacking formation is still 20 kilometres ($12\frac{1}{2}$ miles) from the Forward Edge of Battle Area (FEBA). It is essential to start as soon as is feasible, not only to maximise the number of kills before the attacking tanks are close enough to shoot back, but also to force their crews to close their hatches early, with the resulting degradation of efficiency and disruption of formations that severely curtailed visibility can be expected to cause.

Only tube and rocket artillery have this kind of range, and since high-explosive shells will prove ineffective, they will be used to deliver submunitions in the form of mines and hollow-charge bomblets. The mines distributed ahead of the formation are designed to force the tanks to halt while the bomblets are distributed in a dispersed pattern, their small hollow charges being designed to penetrate the tanks' comparatively thin top armour.

Under development are smart submunitions which will be stabilised by parachute after ejection while they use infra-red or millimetre-wave radar seekers to scan for targets: on sensing one, they fire a self-forging

fragment in the target's direction. Similar technology is now being applied to mortar rounds, with the parachute stabilisation replaced by gas jets, rockets or some other means of altering terminal trajectory on sensing a target in order to deliver the warhead vertically on its top. Because of their large diameter compared with bomblets — current rounds correspond to the 81 to 120 mm calibres of standard mortars — these could be useful shaped charges, easily big enough to penetrate top armour, and they could be delivered at mortar ranges of up to 5000 metres (16 400 feet).

Wire-guided anti-tank missiles such the British Swingfire, Franco-German HOT and American TOW have theoretical ranges of up to 4000 metres (13 120 feet), though since they operate on command-to-line-of-sight principles (the operator tracks the target while a sensor in the sight tracks the missile and transmits steering commands to keep it on the line of sight to the target) they are effectively limited to visual range. Weapons such as the Franco-German Milan and American Dragon operate in similar fashion over shorter ranges, and all are armed with hollow-charge warheads.

In order to restore the effectiveness of these warheads against tanks with compound armour, new techniques are being developed. The Swedish Bill is designed to fly one

British Army Air Corps Lynx armed with TOW anti-tank missiles. Attack helicopters represent a formidable opponent for armoured formations but they are compromised by poor bad weather and night flying performance where operations flown using 'nap of the earth' techniques demand exceptional skill. Ultra sophisticated systems such as the US Army's Hughes AH-64A Apache are designed in part to overcome these problems

West German Army Aviation Bo 105 helicopter armed with six HOT wire-guided anti-tank missiles

metre (3 feet 3·37 inches) above the operator's line of sight so as to pass over the top of the tank; a proximity fuze senses the target and fires a shaped charge warhead angled downward at 30 degrees to penetrate the top of the tank, or to reduce the thickness of armour to be penetrated if it hits the angled front. Other efforts are aimed at replacing the guidance wires by fibre optics, or, ideally, dispensing with the command guidance altogether to produce a fire-and-forget weapon.

By the time wire-guided missiles come into play, the advancing armour is likely to be passing over prepared minefields covered by both missiles and friendly tanks dug into prepared firing positions. At this point the mechanised infantry accompanying the attackers are needed to engage the defending anti-tank weapons. The last line of defence comprises shoulder-launched weapons, usually rockets or recoilless guns with a range of 300 metres (985 feet) or so and of which there is a wide variety in service. These are no longer adequate against tank frontal armour, though they are certainly effective against lighter armoured vehicles. Bigger warheads would work, but outsize warheads on existing rockets would have poor flight characteristics, while full-calibre rockets would be cumbersome to transport.

Air Power Versus Armour

Many helicopters are now equipped to carry anti-tank weapons, including cannon, free-flight rockets and guided missiles. Helicopters are generally highly mobile but limited in endurance and, unless they are purpose-built for battlefield combat, their survival chances may not be high. The most formidable anti-tank helicopter in the NATO armoury is the AH-64 Apache, which is fitted with a comprehensive array of target acquisition and attack systems, and delivers a heavy punch.

Basic armament of the Apache is a 30 mm Chain Gun, with 440 rounds of ammunition in the anti-tank role, while pylons on the stub wings carry 16 Hellfire missiles. Unlike the wire-guided TOW and similar weapons carried by most anti-tank helicopters, Hellfire is a laser-guided weapon which homes in on targets designated by the Apache's own, another helicopter's, or a ground-based laser designator. After launch it accelerates rapidly to Mach 1·17 and has a range of six kilometres (3·75 miles). Prior lock-on is not essential, and even in rapid-fire multiple launches the missile has demonstrated an ability to acquire separate targets designated by coded lasers during flight.

The nose of the Apache mounts an array of sensors, including the pilot's forward-looking infra-red (Flir) night vision system. Below this is the target acquisition/designation sight, which incorporates Flir, tv, direct-view optics, laser range-finder/designator and laser spot tracker, and which feeds visual display units in the pilot's and gunner's cockpits and to their integrated helmet and display sight system. This combination provides a range of tactical options and a high degree of accuracy.

Fixed-wing aircraft have a more limited part to play in the anti-armour battle. At the low levels and high speeds necessary for battlefield survival, precise aiming is likely to be extremely difficult, even with the sophisticated navigation and targeting systems now entering production. The only weapon with much chance of hitting a tank is a cluster bomb, which dispenses a large number of submunitions, but these could probably be delivered more cost-effectively by tube or rocket artillery. In any case, the ratio of targets to available air assets on NATO's Central Front is such that aircraft will be in great demand and short supply.

The exception to the above is the only dedicated anti-tank fixed-wing aircraft currently in service, the USAF A-10 Thunderbolt. An outsize wing of six squadrons of these tank-busters is based in England; in a confrontation with the Warsaw Pact these would deploy to six Forward Operating Locations (FOLs) in Germany while reinforcements were flown in from the US. Primary armament of the A-10 is an extremely powerful 30 mm gun which fires depleted uranium bullets at high muzzle velocity and with a correspondingly high degree of accuracy, at a rate of up to 4200 rounds a minute. A one-second burst should put 40 shells into a target the size of two tanks, and with six hits considered a lethal dose, kill probability is high. For survival the A-10 relies on armour protection, systems duplication and excellent agility to stay low, climbing to a maximum of 150 metres (500 feet) to fire its gun and returning to terrain-masking flight at under 30 metres (100 feet) before anti-aircraft guns at its own gun's effective range can hit it.

The other principal weapon carried by the A-10 is the Maverick missile, which can use tv, laser or infra-red guidance, has demonstrated accuracy and carries a powerful shaped-charge warhead. In fact in Israeli service Mavericks have been fired with inert warheads, so that the tanks could be captured rather destroyed, and have succeeded in knocking off turrets through kinetic energy alone. Another weapon proposed for the A-10, the Hypervelocity Missile, also uses kinetic energy, relying on its speed of Mach 4·5 for its destructive effect.

The Warsaw Pact takes the aircraft threat more seriously than NATO appears to, and Soviet armoured formations are liberally provided with anti-aircraft guns and missiles, in addition to their own organic tactical aviation. The US Army is trying to close the gap with the new Sgt York twin 40 mm self-propelled anti-aircraft gun, but despite a wide range of such weapons currently available, few have found their way to front-line anti-tank units.

The absence of integral tactical airpower may well be a more serious drawback in the face of a Warsaw Pact offensive. The US Army has been denied armed fixed-wing aircraft since the US Air Force became an independent service in 1947, and European armies have long ceased to be able to afford such luxuries in army aviation. However, it seems unlikely that an aircraft like the A-10 would be allocated to a separate organisation if planners were starting from scratch, especially in view of new tactics which involve A-10 and Apache working together on the battlefield.

Organic air defence is essential if armoured forces are going to stand a chance against anti-tank helicopters and close support ground attack aircraft. This is the Franco-German Roland 2 short range surface-to-air missile system mounted on a Marder chassis

6 ELECTRONIC WARFARE

Modern weapon systems are designed to apply the appropriate level of destructive force with the maximum efficiency in time and space. The armed forces which employ them themselves depend upon a web of electronic systems to carry out the vitally important tasks of command, control, communications and intelligence to do the same thing. They use radios to transmit orders and to receive intelligence at all levels of command. Radars, infra-red and laser systems are used for surveillance, target acquisition and designation, and weapon guidance. Consequently the side that can deny its opponent full use of the electro-magnetic spectrum, while protecting its own electronic systems from interference, will have gained a potentially decisive advantage. This is why electronic warfare (EW) — and electronic countermeasures (ECM) which strike at the electronic nervous system of the enemy armed forces — have become two of the most complex and fast-changing branches of military technology.

A major British-based company, a leading innovator and manufacturer of EW equipment defined C³I thus — 'the assimilation in one place, of information from all sources to enable a commander to plan his actions, communicate with his forces and remain fully updated, so allowing him to exercise full control over any situation. C³I can be applied to all facets of defence activities in times of both peace and conflict'.

There are few aspects of armed conflict unaffected by electronic warfare. The electronic battlefield extends from under the oceans to outer space, but its impact is probably greatest on the tactical employment of land, sea and air forces.

Electronic warfare can be subdivided into several broad categories. Electronic intelligence (ELINT) is the gathering of information on an enemy's electronic systems as an essential preliminary to planning an ECM campaign against him, quite apart from the intelligence value of the information gleaned. Electronic support measures (ESM) is the use of passive monitoring equipment to detect and identify enemy forces or threats. Any radio or radar transmission can not only give away the position of its user at long range, but by analysing the characteristics of the signals the enemy can determine precisely what military system is transmitting. ECM is the employment of active jamming or deception

Soviet intelligence gathering 'trawlers' are constant shadows of Western fleet manoeuvres, bristling with aerials and antennae to detect communications traffic and the electromagnetic signatures of weapon systems

techniques against enemy electronic systems, while electronic counter-countermeasures (ECCM) are the means used to counteract jamming.

ELINT is the primary building block of electronic warfare — providing the ground rules without which the game cannot be played.

ELINT systems continually monitor hostile activity, recording radar and radio emissions for later classification and analysis by computer. An important consideration is the Elint 'platform', the vehicle that carries the sensors to the appropriate scene of action. Platforms range from airliners, via container trucks to 'trawlers'. In a shooting war the Elint mission becomes more problematic — during the Israeli invasion of southern Lebanon in 1982 for example, drone aircraft were sent over likely SAM sites to draw their fire so that EW aircraft at stand-off range could glean the vital signatures of the ground intercept and the SAM's terminal guidance radars.

Meanwhile airborne Elint platforms operate at the periphery of the rival powers' areas of critical interest.

The US Air Force' primary electronic reconnaissance aircraft are the Boeing RC-135s of the 55th Strategic Reconnaissance Wing based at Offutt Air Force Base, Nebraska, alongside Strategic Air Command's headquarters. These modified Boeing KC-135 Stratotankers are fitted with numerous electronic monitoring systems and they operate on detachment from many parts of the world, including the United Kingdom, Greece, Alaska and Japan. If necessary the 9th Strategic Reconnaissance Wing's Lockheed U-2s and SR-71s can also be fitted with ELINT equipment and these reconnaissance aircraft, unlike the RC-135s which operate as stand-off systems, could overfly enemy territory at extreme altitude.

The US Navy's Atlantic and Pacific Fleets each maintain a single ELINT aircraft squadron, equipped with the EP-3E version of the Orion patrol aircraft and a dwindling number of EKA-3 Skywarriors. The latter started life as a carrier-based nuclear attack aircraft in the 1950s and has been retained in service primarily because of its ability to operate from aircraft carriers at sea.

Other NATO air arms maintain specialised ELINT forces, including the RAF's No 51 Squadron with BAe Nimrod R1s and the West German Navy's 2 staffed Marinefliegergeschwader 3 with Breguet BR 1150 Atlantiques. Both of these units are particularly active over the Baltic Sea monitoring Soviet naval operations. The Soviet Air Force operates such converted transport aircraft as the Anotov An-12 Cub-B and Ilyushin Il-18 Coot-A in this role.

It would be much more militarily useful if ELINT systems could overfly enemy territory, although electronic emissions can be picked up at surprisingly long ranges. The only current ELINT vehicles which can operate over hostile territory with impunity are the Ferret electronic reconnaissance satellites. US ELINT satellites follow a circular orbit some 900 miles above earth and are launched in concert with Big Bird reconnaissance satellites (see Chapter 7), the massive Titan 34D launcher lifting both satellites as a single payload. The usefulness of the Ferrets lies in their ability to locate defence installations, such as the command centres, missile sites and radars of the Soviet air defence network, deep in enemy territory. They are also important in being able to discern the telemetry transmitted by Soviet missiles under test, which after decoding provide vital intelligence data on range and accuracy.

Ships equipped for ELINT can be used to trail naval forces at sea, or they can operate offshore provided that they stay in international waters. Such activity can be hazardous, however, as shown by the fate of the USS *Pueblo* seized by the North Koreans in 1968, or the USS *Liberty* attacked by Israeli aircraft in 1967 both while on electronic intelligence missions. The Soviet Union maintains a large fleet of intelligence-gathering ships (AGIs), some of them based on commercial hull designs such as whalers or trawlers. There are fifteen such ships in the 'Okean' class and a further eight of the more advanced 'Mayak' class in service. Warships taking part in NATO naval exercises can be sure of attracting a shadowing Soviet AGI bristling with electronic sensors.

Ground monitoring stations also have a part to play in the gathering of electronic intelligence. In the United Kingdom the USAF maintains an interception station at RAF

Aircraft are also vital Elint platforms. The Grumman E-2 Hawkeye of the US Navy is a carrier borne early warning aircraft but with its passive detection capability it is also a useful platform for gathering electronic intelligence. In its latest form, the E-2C, it is capable of detecting multiple targets in a three million cubic mile envelope as an AEW aircraft

Inside a NATO operated E-3A Sentry Airborne Warning and Control Aircraft (AWACS). The aircraft has a flight crew of four and up to thirteen systems operators depending on the mission. Primary search radar is the Westinghouse AN/APY-1 with a range of 370 km at 8850 m

Chicksands in Bedfordshire, capable of picking up Warsaw Pact aircraft radio transmissions deep within Eastern Europe. The UK National Security Agency (NSA) station at Menwith Hill, Yorkshire, monitors communications in Eastern Europe. A similar installation is reported to be jointly operated by the United States and the People's Republic of China in western China.

The concept of Electronic Support Measures (ESM) is similar to ELINT in that it makes use of passive monitoring equipment. Where it differs is in the use of information gathered. ESM is used as a tactical system to locate enemy transmissions and is an alternative to visual or radar surveillance and target acquisition. The applications of ESM are numerous on land, sea and air. In anti-submarine warfare for example a patrol aircraft, such as the Nimrod MR Mk 2 or P-3 Orion, fitted with ESM receivers and processors can pick up the radar or radio transmissions of an enemy submarine. Not only can a bearing be taken on the transmission but by reference to a 'threat library' of pre-recorded transmissions (derived from ELINT), the transmitter can be identified. This will not only allow the contact to be classified as friendly or hostile, but will also provide a clue to the submarine's precise identity. ESM equipment can be used in much the same way by air defence forces. The latest generation of Western AEW (airborne early warning) aircraft — the RAF's Nimrod AEW Mk 3 and the USAF and NATO E-3 Sentry — can detect hostile radar *emissions* at ranges where their own self-generated radar coverage would be ineffective.

In naval warfare ESM systems include high frequency direction finding (HF/DF) with its distinctive, cage-like aerial atop the masts of many destroyers and frigates. HF/DF equipment can be used to intercept radio transmissions and take a bearing on them — the bearing can then either be 'run down' by the intercepting warship to make contact with the enemy, or if two sufficiently widely separated warships have intercepted the enemy transmission, its position can be determined by triangulation.

Radar transmissions can be intercepted and used in much the same way. The British Racal Cutlass for example, which can be fitted to any warship including fast patrol boats and submarines, provides automatic analysis and identification of the radar signals intercepted. Automatic analysis will determine the salient characteristics of the transmitting radar, namely its pulse repetition frequency (PRF), PRF jitter, pulse width and scan period. These parameters together with any other available data are then compared with a 'dictionary' of known radar signatures, which is stored on magnetic tape. Up to 2000 signatures may be available for comparison with the intercepted signal and a check can be made in well under a second. The result of the analysis and any identification are presented on an alphanumeric display and the system can be programmed to present up to 300 hostile radar threats in order of priority. Such a threat could be the terminal guidance radar of a sea-skimming missile flashed into the ship's Action Information System so that electronic countermeasures or close-in defence can be initiated. A specialised version such as the Racal Porpoise designed for submarines sorts out specially dangerous threats such as when helicopter or maritime surveillance radars reach a pre-programmed danger level.

ESM systems can thus be used defensively to alert a warship when it is about to come under attack and to provide the basic information necessary to initiate electronic countermeasures. Its offensive applications are passive surveillance and target acquisition. The advantages over an *active* system such as radar are that the enemy is not warned that he has been detected, as he would if he were illuminated by radar and that ESM systems have an effective range that is between two to five times greater than radar's. The disadvantages are that positions fixed from ESM equipment cannot be so precise as those provided by radar and that a hostile vessel which is electronically silent will escape detection unless it comes within visual range.

Information derived from an ESM system such as the US Navy's AN/ALQ-142 lightweight system designed for helicopters, fast patrol boats etc is sufficiently precise to enable the targeting of long-range cruise missiles, or standard air-to-surface missiles. Because an exact bearing measurement can

be taken from the signal picked up during a single scan, even an enemy using his radars only intermittently can be detected with some degree of confidence. The initial contact is likely to be made at a range beyond the radar horizon, but this will be sufficient to program a missile for the boost and midcourse stage of its flight. Terminal homing will be by means of an active guidance system, but by the time that this comes into action, the ship under attack will receive only the shortest of warnings from its own ESM equipment.

Infra-red and electro-optical systems can also contribute to ESM in passive detection and target acquisition, but their drawback is limited range. However, they do have some useful applications, as an infra-red sensor can be used to pick up a hostile missile without using a transmitter which the missile could then home on to. Similarly, an interceptor aircraft operating in heavy electronic countermeasure jamming could use an electro-optical telescope (such as the USAF's TISEO or the US Navy's TCS) for target acquisition beyond the pilot's unassisted range of vision.

Battlefield target location by means of ESM techniques is the function of the Precision Location/Strike System (PLSS), which is being developed for use from the TR-1 surveillance aircraft. The primary objectives of the PLSS are the enemy radars which control anti-aircraft artillery (AAA) and surface-to-air missiles (SAMs). Operating as a stand off platform in friendly territory, the high flying PLSS-equipped TR-1 is designed to detect enemy radar emissions and transmit an accurate bearing and distance measurement to a ground-based computerised processing centre. There the data can be translated to identify the target and pinpoint its position, perhaps using information from more than one TR-1. This intelligence will then be

Above: *The mast-mounted antenna array of the AN/SLQ-32 naval electronic warfare system aboard a US warship. The system is modular with three variants of increasing capability. The most capable fitted to ships of cruiser size and above can identify hostile transmissions and actively jam them.* **Right:** *The SLQ-32 control station where the first indication of an incoming anti-ship missile would show up*

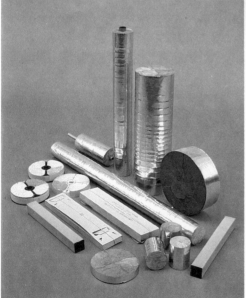

*'Chaff' is one of the simplest yet most effective of electronic countermeasures strewing millions of tiny reflectors in the path of a hostile acquisition radar. This is what the so called 'roving', usually metallicised glass fibre, looks like close up with (**left**) some of the forms it comes in before dispensing*

relayed to a tactical air control centre, which can direct an airstrike against the target, assisted by navigational data from the PLSS. Detection and location can be achieved in seconds and an air attack mounted soon after a radar starts transmitting. The PLSS represents a vital component of the whole 'deep strike' concept of warfare.

The location of hostile transmitters on the battlefield does not necessarily require such sophisticated equipment as the TR-1/PLSS combination. Signals intelligence (SIGINT) and ESM equipment may be carried by light aircraft, such as the US Army's RU-21J. Alternatively it can be ground based, either mounted in vehicles or in fixed stations. Lightweight high-frequency radio direction-

The Beech RU-21J is operated by the US Army as part of a Sigint programme called Guardrail. Aircraft fly along hostile borders picking up signals traffic at long range

finding equipment can even be man-portable.

SIGINT is the building up of the enemy's electronic order of battle through both communications intercepts (COMINT) and the monitoring of other electronic transmissions via ELINT. As various types and combinations of electronic equipment are associated with specific military units (for example the radio and radar emissions produced by an armoured division will be different from that of a mechanised infantry division), much information of general military and political intelligence value can be gleaned from SIGINT. Furthermore, as certain patterns of signal traffic may precede a particular enemy activity, by employing the techniques of signals traffic analysis, advanced information of enemy intentions may be gained. If the enemy is so lax in communications security as to allow his radio messages to be decrypted, then of course the intelligence haul will be so much the greater. As in other applications, ground-based ESM are concerned with identifying and locating hostile transmitters, which can then be attacked.

Representative of numerous ground-based systems is the US Army's AN/MSQ-103A Teampack Radar Monitoring System, which can be mounted on a tracked vehicle, utility truck or even a jeep. The system can detect both air defence and artillery radars. The British Racal System 3000 can be built up from modular units into either a fixed-base monitoring station, or truck-mounted to provide a mobile tactical ESM detachment — perhaps linked to a fixed station in the army's rear area.

Electronic Countermeasures

ECM is where electronic warfare comes alive, when the activities of ELINT, SIGINT, electronic support measures and the rest are turned into actual combat power by striving to reduce or indeed exploit the effectiveness of hostile electromagnetic radiation. ECM can be passive or active ranging from a relatively simple self defence measure, to a large scale attack on an enemy's entire electronic nervous system using deep ranging destructive weapons such as anti-radiation missiles (ARMS) as well as jammers.

In air warfare for example a combat aircraft faces a threat from rival interceptors with airborne radar, air-to-air missiles with either heat-seeking or radar guidance, ground intercept radar controlling surface-to-air missiles and radar-directed anti-aircraft artillery (AAA). A missile's homing head may be clever but it cannot as yet see or recognise its target in a real sense — its sensors tell its on-board computer that there is a heat source out there or a big metallic reflector or radar returns. The simplest form of defensive ECM therefore is to present it with a dummy target, a cloud of 'chaff', an infra-red flare or an 'expendable' dummy source of electronic emissions. 'Chaff' (developed by the British during the Second World War as a means of counteracting German ground radars and codenamed 'window') is dispensed as a cloud of metallic foil strips which will act as a source of radar reflection. Ideally they should act as miniature dipoles with a length equal to the wavelength of the hostile emitter. Rapid blooming is essential so chaff in most applica-

The chaff rocket system called Shield has been developed for small warships. Such systems are a last ditch defence against the threat of the sea-skimming anti-ship missile aiming to present a false target to its terminal guidance radar

tions is fired from a dispenser by a cartridge to burst and bloom into a cloud in under two seconds.

Airborne self-defence ECM systems can be mounted internally or as external stores and often incorporate other types of counter-measures for dealing with the heat-seeking missile threat as well as radar-confounding chaff. The Tracor ALE-39 ECM dispenser for example equipping US Navy aircraft carries chaff cartridges, IR flares and expendable jammers, loaded in any combination in multiples of ten, either dispensable singly on command or automatically according to preset programs and inputs from the aircraft's threat warning systems.

A different sort of system is the ALE-43 chaff cutter dispenser pod manufactured by Lundy which, instead of firing a bloom of chaff, dumps a continuous stream into the air flow. The advantage is that the chaff 'roving' (the name for the continuous strips of metal-licised foil) can be automatically cut to the dipole length of the hostile emitter's frequency for maximum efficiency.

Naval chaff rockets are designed to function against anti-ship missiles but have a greater range and are able to provide something like a 'layered' defence. The British 'Barricade' system for example consists of multiple rocket launchers positioned in two sets of eighteen to provide all-round coverage of a warship with short-, medium- and long-range rockets. The system can operate in the following modes: Confusion — long-range rockets fired to confuse enemy search radar; Distraction — medium-range chaff and infra-red flare rockets fired in patterns of six around the ship to present a multiplicity of targets to incoming missiles during their search phase; Dump — if a missile has locked on to a ship and its range gate has been stolen by a jammer, the gate may be dumped onto a chaff cloud allowing the jammer to be switched to another threat; Centroid — this is a last ditch defence against a single missile which has locked on.

A pattern of chaff is bloomed rapidly to create a large alternative and hopefully highly attractive target down range of the ship which will take evasive action to escape. The missile's seeker head locks on the 'centroid' (the apparent centre of mass) and is decoyed away. The missile however is not destroyed by its encounter with a chaff cloud — it will continue its flight until burn out or until it picks up another target. This is what happened to the *Atlantic Conveyor* during the Falklands sea combat when two Exocets aimed at *HMS Hermes* were successfully deflected by the carrier but picked up the container ship instead.

The US Navy's equivalent system is called RBOC (Rapid Bloom Off Board Countermea-

Above: Electronic warfare has its dramatic moments as evidenced by this Chinook helicopter firing infra-red decoy flares, a defence against surface-to-air heat-seeking missiles

sures) which, as well as chaff fires an infra-red system called HIRAM (Hycor Infra-red Anti-missile). When fired, a flare is deployed with a parachute and float, burning intensely in the air or on water and simulating the radiant intensity of the largest ship. While decoys present a missile's guidance system with false information, exploiting the efficiency of its sensors but the inadequacy of its discriminatory intelligence, the second major aspect of passive electronic countermeasures is to degrade the efficiency of its sensors by 'jamming' — or obliterating the hostile emission by generating powerful transmissions on the

same wavelength. Sheer brute strength is one solution, pumping out powerful signals in all directions over the entire spread of frequencies over which a threat might operate, but this requires a large input of power itself and strenuous efforts to keep equipment cool.

For applications on aircraft this represents a critical problem thus a state-of-the-art airborne jamming system will incorporate a computer-controlled power management system. This will concentrate on the hostile transmitter's bandwidth, picked up and analysed by an internal receiver/processor, and has a look-through ability to allow continuous surveillance of the radar environment while jamming is in progress.

So called 'deception' jamming is another solution showing off the cut and thrust of the electronic duel to effect. A hostile radar will illuminate its target with energy and the processed signal returns provide the information for target acquisition and weapon guidance. These transmissions can however be exploited by employing a transponder (transmitter/responder) to operate each time it receives a pulse of energy from a hostile emitter. The pulses returned can be smaller, larger or out of synchronisation with the hostile signals so the searching radar will be bent off course.

In aircraft applications, jammers can be pod mounted giving tactical aircraft their own flexible ECM capability, built into the airframes of high-cost, high-performance aircraft, or installed in special-purpose electronic warfare aircraft assigned to fly composite combat missions and provide powerful ECM coverage against ground-based air defence. The US Navy has deployed the Grumman EA-6B Prowler since the end of the Viet Nam War as its primary shipborne elec-

The Grumman EA-6B Prowler is the US Navy's primary carrier borne electronic warfare aircraft with a four-man crew and the AN/ALQ-99 tactical jamming system pod mounted under the wings powered by wind-driven turbo-generators

tronic warfare aircraft, with a useful secondary ELINT capability. The heart of the system is the AN/ALQ-99 tactical jamming system comprising receiving sensors, a central processor, a powerful IBM AYQ-6A computer and transmitters housed in five external pods and powered by wind-driven turbo-generators. In addition the EA-6B carries a chaff/flare dispenser, surface to air missile launch warning system, radar rack breaker and airborne communications jammer.

The US Navy's Prowlers have been subject to a continuous update and improvement process allowing the electronics to remain at the state-of-the-art within the same basic airframe and able to provide electronic warfare support for fleet air defence as much as for penetrating strike groups of carrier aircraft.

The ALQ-99 system provides the basis for the USAF's equivalent electronic warfare aircraft, the Grumman EF-111 Raven derived from the variable General Dynamics F-111 fighter bomber. The Ravens are designed to provide electronic support to USAF combat aircraft in the toughest of combat environments such as those which could be expected on NATO's Central Front. The ALQ-99E

The EF-111A Raven is the US Air Force's equivalent of the Prowler but based on the airframe of the F-111 and capable of supersonic speeds. The AN/ALQ-99E jamming system is mounted in pallets in the weapons bay (above) and has a single operator

jamming system is mounted internally with ten transmitters mounted in the former bomb bay with an aerial array in an under-belly 'canoe' housing. Increased computer power allows a single operator instead of the EA-6B's three and a greatly enlarged 'threat library'.

Infra-red seeker heads can also be jammed. The US Navy's ALQ-123 system for example is designed for pod mounting on ground attack aircraft affording protection against short-range IR homing surface-to-air missiles such as the SA-7 Grail. The ram air turbine driven system generates a series of intense light pulses coded to break the lock of an IR seeker.

US Army helicopters, again particularly vulnerable to heat-seeking SAMs, use electrically heated ceramic bricks, mechanically modulated to generate jamming signals.

Jamming also has shipborne and land-based applications. US carriers for example are equipped with the highly capable AN/SLQ 17 naval ECM Suite developed by the Hughes Aircraft Company, with threat warning receivers and jamming transmitters positioned on each side of the ship and the controlling computer and operator's station located at the heart of the warship's combat information centre. The system can detect and track the signals of a large number of hostile missiles and will track several hundred signals from other platforms. The system keeps track of any navigation and search emissions in the frequency bands of

known potentially hostile platforms — that is the ship or aircraft which might fire a missile at the target, and it can intercept and identify these threats beyond the ranges at which any missiles launched could lock onto the ship. If a signal is received, the SLQ-17 automatically assesses its characteristics, and compares them with information stored in its 'threat library' to see what sort of missile it is and whether it is hostile. If so, the system operates in the deception jamming mode, to return false signals on the hostile emitter's wavelength, offsetting the return of the ship itself thus steering the missile harmlessly into the ocean.

EW on the land battlefield shows a different emphasis to air and sea applications, where generally speaking the emphasis is on self protection for high value targets against radar directed threats. Land-based EW tends to be offensive in nature with enemy tactical communications as the target. The land battlefield commander has to gain a temporary or localised advantage which he can exploit with firepower and reserves to get leverage — in this situation EW actions against rival command, control and communications networks (while striving to protect one's own) are more critical than radar-oriented electronic warfare.

The Soviet Union has made a speciality of ground-based electronic warfare systems aimed at compromising the West's more technology-intensive defence. The capability for 'radioelectronic combat' as the Soviets call it, is found throughout the Soviet Army, not just within specialised units, and is judged by professional observers to have a formidable effectiveness. Soviet EW capability includes the interception and analysis of hostile radar and radio transmissions, jamming and counter-countermeasures. It includes radio direction-finding equipment to acquire order of battle intelligence and tactical targeting data, and jamming to blanket hostile electronic equipment which cannot be destroyed by direct means. Personnel are also trained in breaking into enemy communications nets and broadcasting falsified orders.

The Soviet Army's own signals technology and practices are comparatively crude compared with their Western counterparts but although this means tactical inflexibility, it is also less vulnerable itself to electronic warfare. A Motor Rifle company's commander for example would only be netted into other company commanders, the vehicles under his control and higher command. Requests for support from other units or target reports would have to be relayed up the chain of command before being acted upon although there are procedures to short-circuit this cumbersome structure. Much use is made of runners, hand signals and flares for example, all of course immune to EW; individual tank radios are set to receive only, transmitting only in an emergency. By contrast a US tank company operates on four internal radio nets plus a fifth battalion net making their operational efficiency much more vulnerable to effective electronic warfare.

Another important component of EW is direct attack by physically destructive systems which use the source of hostile emissions as their source of guidance. The United States Air Force developed specialised 'Wild Weasel' defence-supression aircraft based on various airframes during the Viet Nam War with North Vietnamese air defence radars as their target. Once a signal was acquired, an Anti-Radiation Missile (such as Shrike or Standard) would be launched to fly down the beam and destroy the radar or SAM site. Even if it only caused the radar to be switched off in self defence, at least the air defences were degraded in effectiveness.

The principal SAM supression aircraft in the USAF inventory is the F-4G Phantom, modified from standard F-4E airframes to carry the APR-38 detection system. This can locate and classify sources of hostile emissions (comparing them with its ELINT-derived threat library) and display them in order of threat intensity on the backseater electronic warfare officer's (EWO's) display. The antenna/receiver systems are installed in the

Helicopters are particularly vulnerable to heat-seeking surface-to-air missiles. This US Army AH-1J Cobra has an AN/ALQ 144 infra-red countermeasures system consisting of an electrically-heated ceramic heat source surrounded by a modulation system designed to throw a heat-seeking SAM off the track, mounted directly above the engine exhaust

aircraft nose and the tip of the fin.

Current generation missiles can operate against different frequency bands but have to be pre-programmed before flight. The new generation Texas Instruments AGM-88 HARM (High Speed Anti-Radiation Missile) can be automatically programmed by the APR-38 in flight, can be fired off axis from the target, and is significantly faster than the missiles it replaces giving the target radar less of a chance to shut down in self defence. Self defence ARMs are becoming a vital weapon load component of any combat aircraft which has to penetrate hostile air defence and Royal Air Force Tornados are due to receive a British developed defence suppression mis-

Self defence jamming pods are now a vital part of a combat aircraft's weapons load. The Italian Elettronica ELT/555 jammer is seen here carried by a Macchi MB 339 strike/trainer

sile called Alarm. The USAF meanwhile is working on a lightweight, low cost missile for simpler tactical aircraft and helicopters based on the Sidewinder AAM called Sidearm.

While the primary targets of aircraft such as the EF-111A and the F-4G Wild Weasel are air defence radars, the USAF also has a programme called Compass Call in which the target is hostile communications networks. Based in EC-130H modified Hercules aircraft, powerful jammers would be flown at stand off range orbiting within friendly territory to disrupt rival C^3 nets. A ground based system aimed at hostile *airborne* communications and radar systems is called Comfy Challenge.

Counter-countermeasures

The electronic battle does not end with ECM. The counter to ECM is naturally enough electronic counter-countermeasures (ECCM) which uses an enormously wide range of techniques to reduce the susceptibility of radar and radio equipment to jamming or deception. ECCM can be incorporated into equipment at the design stage — for example by employing a technique known as frequency agility, where the electromagnetic emission is rapidly switched at random from frequency to frequency. Similarly, the ECCM technique of jittered pulse repetition frequency seeks to defeat jamming by making random variations in the radar's pulse repetition period. A radar set's transmitted pulses must be spaced to allow for the reception of a return signal — however there is no reason why the pulses should be transmitted in a regular pattern, which can be anticipated and exploited by deception jamming.

Another way of building increased ECM resistance into a radar set is by 'sidelobe suppression'. This technique aims at reducing that part of the radar beam which is off the main lobe (that is that area of the sky which the radar wishes to survey). This is a necessary measure because an ECM operator can use a hostile radar's sidelobe to produce a deceptive return signal which will mislead the radar about its target's true bearings and break the lock-on.

Making communications networks resistant to eavesdropping and jamming is another important thrust of ECCM technology. The United States' armed forces are working towards an ambitious 'multiple access information distribution system' designed to be as jam resistant as technically possible, yet remain a high capacity communications network for all kinds of mobile users ranging from AWACS aircraft to dispersed units in the field. It is known as JTIDS (Joint Tactical Information Distribution System) and can transmit either voice communications or pulsed bursts of 'digitalised' information including navigation and IFF (identification friend or foe) data working within the 960 to 1215 MHz band.

The key to the system is the employment of the technique called 'Time Division Multiple Access'. Security is safeguarded by the use of spread-spectrum, frequency-hopping trans-

Above: *MBB concept for an electronic warfare dedicated Tornado strike aircraft. As well as Kormoran anti-shipping missiles below the fuselage, High Speed Anti-Radiation Missiles (HARM) are carried on inner wing pylons with pod-mounted ECM equipment on the outer wing pylons*

Left: *Not an electronic warfare system as such but a force enhancer dependent on electronics and a likely target for EW itself is this Hughes Firefinder radar. It can back plot the trajectory and launch position of incoming mortar and artillery shells*

Right: *'TPZ-1 Eloka' or armoured electronic combat system based on the Thyssen-Henschel Transportpanzer-1 of the West German Army*

missions which can be encrypted. This inhibits following of the signals by an uninvited intruder but virtually eliminates the possibility of their being successfully jammed.

A JTIDS transmission has an electronic lock at its beginning which must be opened for access. The initial pulses of a JTIDS transmission are called the 'synchronisation members' which lock the individual transmission equipment to the frequency-hopping sequence of the entire system. Immediately behind these come a series of pulses confirming the *user's* identity and not until both synchronisation and identification pulses have been respectively locked on can the transmission become interpretable. The Time Division Multiple Access technique splits transmission time up into 12-second cycles, each reserved for different classes of user such as air-to-air, air-to-warship and so on. Each 12-second cycle is further subdivided into 1536 slots of 7·8 milliseconds each, even one single slot capable of imparting a large degree of digitalised information.

The infantryman of the 1980s is himself a component of the battle for the electromagnetic spectrum. Systems such as the Hughes Position Locating Reporting System presage the day when every soldier will be hooked up to remote computers

A GLOSSARY OF ELECTRONIC WARFARE

Absorbtive Chaff: Also called 'black chaff' — designed to absorb rather than reflect electromagnetic emissions.

Agility: Ability of a radar to change randomly its parameters — frequency, pulse width, pulse reception frequency, without reducing its operational performance.

Burnthrough: The appearance of a true target on a radar indicator or other detection device in a jamming environment.

Chaff: Light airborne reflectors, usually made of aluminium or zinc-coated glass fibre able to reflect radar emissions.

Chaff Receiver: ECCM technique — an auxiliary receiver switched into the radar system which uses the chaff return signal as its reference, detecting true moving targets within it.

COMINT: Communications Intelligence, data derived from analysis of hostile signals traffic.

Command Guidance: Intelligence transmitted to a missile or vehicle from an outside source, commanding it to traverse a directed flight path.

Conformal Antenna: Antenna or receiver built into the airframe or structure of the system carrying it.

Deception ECM: The intentional transmission or retransmission of amplitude, frequency, phase or otherwise modulated intermittent or continuous wave signals for the purpose of misleading hostile electronic systems.

Doppler Effect: The frequency shift of propagated energy due to relative motion between transmitter or receiver and the medium in which the signal is propagated. Doppler target recognition is an ECCM technique using Doppler effect to distinguish true targets from jam, chaff or clutter.

Duty-cycle: The ratio between a transmitted pulse width and its corresponding pulse repetition period.

ELINT: Electronic Intelligence. The analysed and codified results of electronic reconnaissance.

ESM: Electronic Support Measures. Systems for the identification and analysis of hostile electro-magnetic emissions for immediate tactical purposes.

Frequency: The number of cycles per second between a positive and negative value produced in the electromagnetic medium.

Frequency Band: Continuous range of frequencies extending between two limiting values — measured in Hertz (Hz) 1 Hz = 1 cycle per second.

Frequency bands — current NATO designations

BAND	FREQUENCY	WAVELENGTH
HF	10–30 MHz	30–10 m
VHF	30–100 MHz	10–3 m
A Band	100–300 MHz	3–1 m
B Band	300–500 MHz	1·25m–60 cm
C Band	0·5–1 GHz	60–30 cm
D Band	1·0–2·0 GHz	30–15 cm
E Band	2·0–3·0 GHz	15–10 cm
F Band	3·0–4·0 GHz	10–7·5 cm
G Band	4·0–6·0 GHz	7·5–5 cm
H Band	6·0–8·0 GHz	5–3·75 cm
I Band	8·0–10·0 Ghz	3·75–3 cm
J Band	10·0–20·0 GHz	3–1·5 cm
K Band	20·0–40·0 GHz	1·5–0·75 cm
L Band	40·0–60·0 GHz	0·75–0·5 cm
M Band	60·0–100 GHz	0·5–0·3 cm

Gate stealing: ECM technique that repeats a large jamming signal back to the victim radar bigger than the defending vehicle's own radar cross-section return. Then it gradually increases or decreases the angle, range or velocity of the jamming signal relative to the *true* signal causing the victim radar's range gate to move away. After a specified walk-off time, the jamming is turned off. The radar then loses track and must go into a search mode again.

IFF: Identification Friend or Foe. A radar transponder programmed to give a coded reply is triggered by a friendly radar.

Jamming, deception: See Deception ECM.

Jamming, noise: Direct noise on a carrier frequency to saturate the receiver of a hostile radar system.

Jamming, spot: Measures on a precise frequency.

Lock-On: Operating mode of many radars in which pencil-beam remains pointing at a target as it moves around.

Modulation: The impression of the essential characteristics of a signal onto a carrier wave.

PRF: Pulse repetition frequency.

RINT: Radiation intelligence

SAR: Synthetic Aperture Radar. Antenna system in which the aperture (the effective area of the antenna for intercepting electromagnetic energy) is 'synthesised' into a much more receptive long aperture by the multiplication of radar returns obtained along the aircraft's flight path.

Sidelobe: Any lobe of a radar transmit/receive pattern not on the main lobe.

SLAR: Sideways Looking Airborne Radar, radar producing a presentation of terrain or moving targets viewed at 90 degrees to the axis of the aircraft.

Transponder: Equipment that transmits a replica of received signals. Can be used for false target generation and for range gate walk-off.

Wavelength: Distance between successive crests along an electromagnetic wave. The greater the wavelength, the lower the frequency.

7 WAR
IN SPACE

Space is not yet a battlefield, but neither is it a sea of tranquillity. In spite of the Outer Space Treaty of 1967 which forbids the signatories to place weapons of mass destruction in orbit, about three-quarters of all earth satellites launched have been for military purposes. The treaty, which entered force in October 1967, left significant loopholes. The key article IV (1) reads: 'Parties to the Treaty undertake not to place in orbit around the earth any objects carrying nuclear weapons or any other kind of weapons of mass destruction, install such weapons on celestial bodies or station such weapons in outer space in any other manner'. While this high minded agreement was meant to rule out the possibility of nuclear, chemical or biological weapons being placed in 'storage' orbits and called down on command, it did not necessarily proscribe the placing in orbit of 'tactical' space systems capable of attacking each other — rival satellites for example, nor weapons which would enter space en route to their targets, such as ICBMs or the Soviet FOBS (Fractional Orbital Bombardment System) 'wrong way round the globe' rockets.

By the early 1970s the Soviets had successfully tested low altitude killer satellites able to close in on a target in orbit and explode close enough to destroy it. The USA began testing a low altitude anti-satellite missile in 1982. ASAT (anti-satellite) technology failed to be proscribed meanwhile by fitful arms control diplomacy in the late 1970s but by the mid-eighties the ASAT issue had been overshadowed by the far greater technological and political conundrum of a space based 'defence' against ballistic missiles using directed energy weapons — the so called 'Star Wars' issue.

But 'tactical' space weapons such as ASATs are of great significance because they are designed to attack the strategic space systems, which although not weapons as such, are vitally important in animating and informing the weapons of mass destruction that wait on earth. The nuclear world order of today would be impossible without space systems. The very concept of deterrence begins and ends with the idea of 'warning' — an inbound attack should be verified in enough time for an assured retaliatory attack to be made. Kick away the command, control and communications (C^3) and deterrence no longer works — early warning and the C^3 net begins and ends with space-based systems for its execution and for nuclear war planning.

Intelligence and reconnaissance satellites with their super accurate mapping have been instrumental in leading strategic targeting doctrines away from the idea of 'mutual assured destruction', which depended on tar-

geting sprawling area — targets such as cities, to 'counterforce' strategies based on pinpoint precision targeting of rival weapon systems and control centres. The TERCOM (terrain contour mapping) guidance system by which the apparently 'cheap' US cruise missiles in their various forms navigate with great accuracy depends on satellite mapping. The same is true for the submarine-launched ballistic missiles of the Trident 2 generation which are as accurate as their land-based counterparts, a fact made possible by space-based artificial guidance reference points for the launch submarine and for mid-course correction, and geophysical information on the earth's gravitational field.

A global superpower like the United States cannot run its world spanning military machine without space-based intelligence and communications systems. The British forces engaged in the Falklands fighting of 1982 would have found it much tougher going without access to US space-based fleet communications and reconnaissance systems. The Soviet Union, first in space with Sputnik 1 in 1957, has unremittingly used space as a means of staking its claim to be a global superpower and to subject the United States to the prospect of direct strategic attack.

Thus space is and has long been a fundamentally important military arena. At the start of the 1980s several factors combined to make it an even bigger international issue. First were the vocal reports in the West of the Soviets' ability to knock out US satellites with their co-orbital hunter killers, testing of which restarted in 1976. Second was the development of a US anti-satellite system (ASAT) based on an aircraft-launched missile and the impact of this programme on arms control diplomacy. Next was the advent of the US Shuttle, overbudget and beset by teething troubles, but still of immense military significance with the US military space budget outstripping the civil agency NASA's. The Soviets, loudly proclaimed meanwhile that the shuttle was a military system. The US Air Force set up its own Space Command in September 1982 with the telling motto 'Guardians of the High Frontier', followed by the US Navy with Naval Space Command (NavSpaCom) in October 1983. Both services are under political pressure to combine resources in a unified tri-service 'Space Command'. Time, and money ($8000 million on 'national security' space spending in 1983), will tell if this becomes a reality.

Much more controversial, and the issue which above all pushed 'space war' into the public consciousness, was the call made by President Reagan in April 1983 for the US

scientific community (and by inference the US and Western alliance taxpayers who would fund them) to develop a space-based system of strategic defence which would replace the doctrine of 'mutually assured destruction' with that of 'assured survival'.

The President's Strategic Defense Initiative (SDI), to give it its official title, should be set however against the background of faltering arms control diplomacy. Hints that it is a way of cowing the Soviets with US technological superiority have been met by warnings that the US should not even contemplate using the SDI as a bargaining ploy at any renewed strategic or theatre nuclear weapons talks, on the grounds that 'there is no prospect whatsoever that science and technology can, at any time in the next several decades, make nuclear weapons impotent and obsolete'. In addition, the President's idea that the US could, at some

time in the future, transfer strategic defensive technology to the Soviets so they too could turn from offensive weapons of deterrence to 'assured survival' passive systems, has been countered by the same commentator with the argument that, 'in the real world any defensive system would be an imperfect complex of technological operational capabilities, full understanding of which would at once enable any adversary to improve his own methods of penetration'.

These are the arguments at the heart of the Strategic Defense Initiative debate. Before looking at how the technology might work it is worth remembering that the prospect of 'assured survival' becoming attainable by either side of the existing deterrent equation is a leap into the nuclear unknown. Furthermore, if effective directed energy weapons are based in space, they might be considered

A laser battle station smiting a hostile satellite, one of the concepts being researched under the Strategic Defense Initiative

Left: *The Shuttle, the United States' re-usable system for launching payloads into low earth orbit. From the mid-1980s the USAF took an increasing slice of the programme with the first classified all-military flight in 1985*

Right: *In contrast the Soviet Union has concentrated on large 'traditional' boosters to put large payloads into orbit. This is a Soyuz launch, the system capable of putting 1100 kg into geostationary orbit or 7500 kg into low earth orbit*

offensive systems able to strike targets on earth such as missile silos or oil tankers as much as defensive systems straining to bring down an ICBM in the first few seconds of its boost phase or swatting down swarms of re-entry vehicles.

Meanwhile satellites are the principle protagonists in military space, broadly fulfilling the following functions: global communications, early warning of long range missile attack (and, in the not too distant future, tactical warnings of low level threats inside the atmosphere), surveillance of events on the ground and at sea, electronic intelligence, weather reconnaissance, navigational reference and position fixing and, on the Soviet side, anti-satellite warfare.

Satellites are not permanent features of the heavens. According to the way they are put into orbit (angle in relation to the earth, height and speed), the track of their orbit can be shaped for the maximum mission effectiveness. Some navigation, communication, surveillance and early warning satellites will be designed for permanence and thus be put into 'geostationary' orbits at an altitude above the equator and at a velocity where the period of orbit will match the earth's rotation, thus the satellite will appear to stand still relative to a point on the earth below. Photo reconnaissance satellites in contrast might be placed into low earth orbit lasting a matter of days reaching their perigee (the lowest point of the orbit) over the area of maximum inter-

est for a close look.

These networks require careful building and rebuilding of their 'architecture' as the orbits decay and systems malfunction or wear out. This is the military significance of the Shuttle which is able not only to place systems in orbit, but to tend them afterwards and conceivably to disable or capture rival systems. The Shuttle can put nearly 30 000 kilograms of useful load into a 1100-kilometre orbit. A joint NASA/US DoD committee was set up in 1982 to investigate the technology required (such as strap-on rockets and 'space tugs') to boost Shuttle payloads into higher orbits.

The US Joint Chief claims that the Soviets are building a Shuttle-type vehicle with double the payload. The configuration is reported to be broadly similar except that the main engines are on the external tank instead of on the orbiter itself. This means that unless the large external tank is recoverable, the engines would be lost each mission, thus increased payload comes at a price.

'Traditional' boosters meanwhile will continue to have an important role to play. Alarmed at setbacks in the Shuttle programme, the US Air Force has pressed for the big Titan 3 booster to be put back into production and there have been proposals that an emergency system for rebuilding nuclear war fighting networks in space should be part of the MX intercontinental ballastic missile (ICBM) programme. The Soviet Union so far has used boosters based on early ICBM designs. The A2 is derived from the early 1960s vintage SS-6 *Sapwood* ICBM with a 7-tonne payload, and the F-1 is based on the SS-9 which is able to put a 4-tonne payload into low orbit.

Reports of a giant Soviet booster began in the late 1960s and were revived by the US Department of Defense in 1983. Lift off thrust was estimated at up to nine million pounds and the system was reported as capable of putting a massive 150 tonnes into a 180-kilometre orbit.

An equally important aspect of military space is the 'ground segment', the control and monitoring infrastructures here on earth. The United States began to develop the ability to watch events in space in the late 1950s, the pace of development made urgent by the Soviets' new found ability to make strategic attacks with first generation nuclear-armed ICBMs which could come over the Arctic to attack the heartland of America. The result was the development of the first early-warning satellite programmes (Midas and Samos) and the building of the Ballistic Missile Early Warning system (BMEWS) with main sites in Alaska, Greenland and Britain feeding information on Soviet rocket launch activity to the underground HQ of North American Aerospace Defense Command (NORAD) in Colorado. Ironically the first US reconnaissance satellites showed how over-dramatised the 'missile gap' scare of the late 1950s had been.

By the early 1970s the short amount of warning time that the land-based BMEWS afforded seemed irrelevant in the age of satellites but the powerful radars have found a new role in tracking satellites and monitoring the re-entry of space debris. (As much to predict the fall of intelligence-rich material as to distinguish the re-entry of a decaying satellite from a multiple warhead attack.)

Similarly the US Pave Paws submarine-launched missile warning system, which covers the Pacific and Atlantic seaboards of the United States, feeds data to the Consolidated Space Operations Center (CSOC) of NORAD.

From CSOC, on current planning, the US Air Force's Space Command, as well as operating the satellite systems looked at later, will have responsibility for the its expanding ground-based space surveillance network. The principle component of this 'Spacetrack' system, operational since 1969, is the big FPS 65 phased radar based at Eglin AFB, Florida. Florida was chosen as the site because most space objects pass within its range every day. This very big radar is highly distinctive, a great block of concrete like a bisected pyramid, one face inclined at a 45-degree angle to

the horizon, facing south across the Gulf of Mexico. Two arrays, transmit and receive, sit side by side, each made up of thousands of individual antennae. Peak power is 32 MW but radiated energy can be varied to suit various targets in space, the whole operation being controlled by two powerful IBM 360/65 computers. These are programmed to carry in their memory orbital details of known space objects and thus be able to isolate any new object or event in space very rapidly, NORAD's 'Resident Space Object Catalogue' currently identifies more than 800 man-made objects in deep space orbit.

Another phased array radar codenamed Cobra Dane is based at Shemya AFB in the Aleutian Islands and, as well as providing early warning and spacetrack functions, this large and powerful radar surveys a 2000-mile 'corridor' covering the primary Soviet missile test range, to glean important telemetry data on the range and accuracy of any new missiles. There are further detection tracking radars in the spacetrack system based in Turkey, Thailand, South Korea, Italy and New Zealand. These are supplemented by the GEODSS (Ground-Based Electro-Optical Deep Space Surveillance System) which tracks and catalogues space objects using very powerful Baker Nunn cameras able to discern objects 5500 kilometres from earth. Three sites in New Mexico, Hawaii and Korea were operational in 1983 with two more by 1987.

Also feeding into the Consolidated Space Operation Center is the US Navy's NAVS-PASUR Line (Navy Space Surveillance System). This detects and tracks satellites passing through an electronic 'fence' strung across the southern United States. Other sensors feeding into the system are the missile test range radars at Vandenberg AFB, on Kwajalein Atoll and Ascension and the UK's Malvern radar.

The Soviet Union established a separate dedicated space defence organisation (PKO) in the early 1960s, and at the same time began to establish its own ground-based strategic warning system. The equivalent of BMEWS is the series of large radars, codenamed 'Hen' by NATO, with sites covering ICBM or SLBM attack from across the Arctic, from south, east and west of the USSR. In 1983 the US Department of Defense released details of a large phased-array radar in central Siberia which was thought to part of an anti-ballistic missile system. Without the equivalent of the US global network of monitoring stations, the Soviet Union also deploys a number of 'space event' ships equipped with antennae and control rooms for monitoring satellite movements. There are at least eleven such vessels the largest being the 45 000-ton *Kosmonaut Yuri Gagarin*.

Right: *FPS-65 radar at Eglin AFB Florida, principal component of the USAF's 'spacetrack' System*

Reconnaissance Satellites

One of the oldest military functions is reconnaissance and the potential of an all-seeing eye in space was obvious from the beginning of post war rocket development. In the US, contracts for a 'strategic' satellite system were put to tender by the Central Intelligence Agency in 1955, with Lockheed winning a development order for the Agena, an upper stage rocket which itself goes into orbit. Since 1959 over 300 Agena flights have been made, a large proportion of them classified military missions. The Big Bird and KH11 spy satellites (see later), for example, are Agena derivatives. The current Agena D has a restartable liquid propellant rocket engine permitting orbit changes on command.

The first operational US photo reconnaissance satellite was Tiros 1 in April 1960 (in fact based on an experimental NASA weather satellite), the first Soviet one was Cosmos 4 two years later. Today's generation have reached a high level of sophistication but are still broadly of two distinct types, 'area sur-

Left: *Construction work under way at Vandenberg AFB California, principal operations centre of the USAF's military space programme*

vey' and 'close look'. As a rule, area survey data is transmitted digitally by radio, providing a low definition first pass over areas of interest. Anything which might require closer examination is covered by a close look, low altitude system using film processed on board and dropped off in recoverable capsules.

The United States began development of the film recovery technique with the Discoverer series. The US Air force directed the programme from Vandenberg AFB from 1959 onwards and, in spite of serious failures, the in-flight recovery technique was proven. However, after a subsequent series of failures, further Discoverer missions were classified. The Samos (Satellite and Missile Observation System) series became operational at the same time but used the technique of video recording TV pictures taken over

'hostile' territory and transmitting them while over the USA. The last of the series was orbited in May 1972 with a life of 80 days, compared with the 20 days of the first of the series, and infra-red scanners for night-observation. At least 19 of the Samos series also carried so-called 'ferret' sub-satellites used to identify targets for subsequent electronic intelligence (Elint) ferrets, whose role and technology is looked at later.

The most significant reconnaissance satellite is the so-called 'Big Bird' series developed by Lockheed's Space and Missile Division. It weighs over 13 000 kilograms as orbited, and consists of a modified Agena upper stage over 15 metres long and 3·05 metres in diameter. Big Bird combines the characteristic functions of the area survey and close look types of reconsat (reconnaissance satellites). The fact that it has a rocket engine, restartable on command means it can stay in low earth orbit much longer than would normally be possible with such a large vehicle encountering drag at such low altitude (10 days maximum extended to 190).

Big Bird is a flying photo laboratory. It carries a very high resolution Perkin-Elmer camera capable of identifying objects as small as 0·3 metre across from heights of up to 160 kilometres. Film is either processed on board, scanned and then transmitted digitally to a global network of seven receiving stations, or it is ejected in capsules which are caught in mid-air by specially modified US Air Force C-130 Hercules aircraft.

The operational technique is similar to that of earth resources satellites. The chosen orbit will be 'sun synchronous' thus it will pass over the same target every day at the same time, making before and after comparisons of activity on the ground in identical lighting condition easier. Similarly, passes might be timed when sun angles are greatest, giving

the extra definition of long shadows. By the end of 1984 eighteen Big Bird launches had been identified; twice yearly launches in the early 1970s dropped to occasional launches to support KH11 (see later) or other specific missions. During the Falklands crisis for example, a Big Bird was orbited (Big Bird 17, launched May 11 1982, duration 208 days) significantly carrying an Elint 'ferret' sub-satellite which was put into much higher orbit.

In 1976 the first of the next generation US spy satellites was launched, codenamed 'Key-hole'. The KH11 series are placed in higher orbit than Big Bird (up to 500 kilometres), launched from Vandenberg AFB by Titan 34D boosters. They also have restartable manouevring motors able to restore the original orbit on command, so giving a two-year lifetime. KH11 does not use the capsule recovery technique but transmits data in near real time based on digital interpretation of what its high resolution cameras, infra-red sensors and side-looking radar discern. Much of the information on Soviet naval con-

Far Left: *Space based reconnaissance systems have revolutionised intelligence gathering and strategic decision making. Area systems pick up items of interest for low orbit close look satellites to scrutinise in extraordinary detail. This view of the Southern Sinai taken from the Space Shuttle gives just a glimpse of the reconsat's strategic power*

Left: *The Hughes thematic imager from the Landsat earth resources satellite is a close relation of military reconnaissance systems*

struction, new ICBM development, the Black-jack Bomber and SS-20 deployment for example, which politically underwrote the Reagan administration's own strategic weapons modernisation programmes, was gleaned by Keyhole satellites. KH9 is a low-altitude film return spacecraft used only to photograph the highest priority targets. A KH9 was launched on July 31, 1983 to inspect a new Soviet missile radar in central Siberia. KH8 missions are classified. It was reported in early 1984 that production of KH8 and KH9 has been terminated because of heavy cost overrun, while the Soviets had apparently learned how to camouflage certain activities effectively keeping them hidden from prying eyes in the sky.

Soviet Spy Satellites

The Soviets have in fact devoted much of their reconsat activity to finding out just what can be seen from space and how to throw a cloak over it. In September 1980, for example, it was reported that the Soviets had placed SS-20 intermediate range and SS-16 intercontinental range missiles side by side (a KH11 had presumably picked this up) so that their own Cosmos craft could see whether the difference could be discerned and thus make verification of the SALT 2 treaty that much more contentious. The fifth Salyut manned space station was flown over large scale military manoeuvres in Siberia in 1976 to assess the practicability of crewed military reconnaissance missions. The Americans reported that Salyut 3, orbited in July 1974, experimented with film ejection and recovery techniques and that special targets had been laid out at the Tyrutam launch centre for the crew to observe.

The three military Salyut missions (the first failed before it became operational) were experimental. The Soviet Union has however flown a very large number of reconsat missions using over six hundred of the Cosmos series with launches of the latest generation averaging some 35 a year in the 1980s. The large number is a reflection of both Soviet dependence on direct photo reconnaissance rather than transmitted digital data, and shorter orbital lives ranging from a few days to nine weeks.

Current Cosmos reconsats are powered and said to be highly manoeuvrable — when weather satellites report the target area to be clear of cloud, a Cosmos can be manoeuvred to an orbit of 150 kilometres or less over the targets during optimum lighting conditions. The large film capsules are not recovered in mid-air but, after parachute descent, are retrieved by special ground search teams.

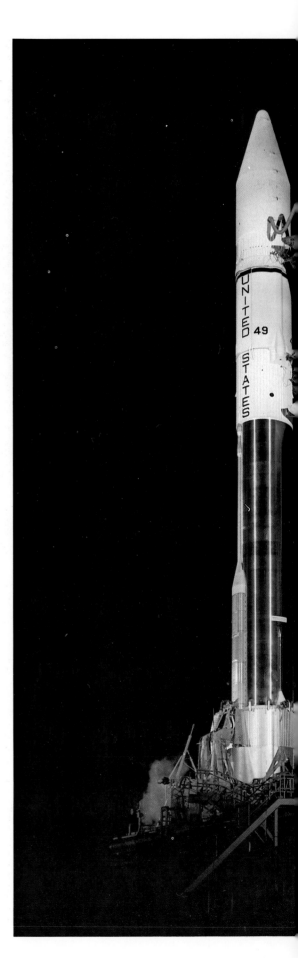

Launch of a US Navy Fleet Communications satellite by Atlas-Centaur booster from Cape Canaveral

Ocean Surveillance Satellites

The big infra-red targets of warships are easier to discern against the background of the oceans than events on land. Ocean reconsats can therefore fly much higher orbits with longer lifetimes than their terrestial counterparts. The US Navy's Ocean Surveillance Satellite for example is equipped with millimetric radar able to track warships through cloud cover plus Elint monitoring devices and can fly orbits up to 1128 kilometres. NOSS 1 launched in April 1976, was observed to release three small sub-satellites into orbits similar to their host's (1092 × 1128 kilometres) with an inclination of 63 degrees and an orbital lifetime of 1600 years. Frequency of launch, however, suggests an operational life of three to five years.

Soviet Radar Equipped Reconnaissance Satellites (Rorsats) began operations in the late 1960s and represent a vital aspect of the Soviet Navy's transformation into a force of global capability. From the early 1970s nuclear-powered Rorsats were launched, usually in pairs, and put into 270-kilometre circular orbits. The Soviet technique involved firing the reactor core into a higher orbit with a 500-year duration at the end of the Rorsat's seventy-day cycle. This complex technique has been far from trouble free — in January 1978 a nuclear-powered Rorsat began to tumble and its orbit to decay before the core could be separated. The eventual re-entry pattern spread nuclear debris over an 800-kilometre strip of northern Canada. (A US Navy nuclear-powered satellite reportedly fell in the Indian Ocean in 1964.) After several further malfunctions, the Soviets used non-nuclear-powered Rorsats but reverted to the original nuclear-powered version in 1980. Two Rorsats were launched in tandem to watch the South Atlantic as the Falklands crisis developed, followed by a pair which operated in the second half of 1982. One of these, C 1402, also malfunctioned but its radioactive power source burned up in re-entry over the south Atlantic.

With the Rorsats the Soviets fly specialised Elint platforms or 'Eorsats' (Electronic Ocean Reconnaissance Satellites) which identify ships, aircraft, radar and missile systems operating below by their electronic 'signatures'. During the movement of the Royal Navy Task Force to the Falklands three Eorsats covered the route. Probably only one was operational, nevertheless electronic silence would have to have been observed as they passed overhead.

Elint Satellites

Eorsats are akin to dedicated Elint (electronic intelligence) satellites generally known as

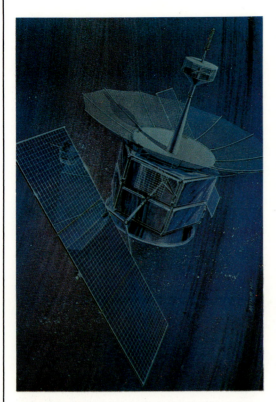

'ferrets'. They are usually placed into higher orbits than photo reconsats and are passive listening devices, picking up the radar signatures of military systems below them. The US Rhyolite 'heavy ferrets' fly geosynchronous orbits, bristling with large antennae, over Soviet rocket test centres at Tyruatum and Plesetsk. Rhyolite is to be replaced by a system called Aquacade which, because of Shuttle delays, has been modified for launch by Titan 34D. A new generation Elint Satellite was the likely payload of the first all-military classified Shuttle mission in 1985.

The Soviets have been flying ferrets since 1970 with an average operational life of $1\frac{1}{2}$ years. They come in two varieties, the first is a network with four launchings a year into a 550-kilometre orbit, with an operational life per satellite of around $1\frac{1}{2}$ years. The second is a larger Elint platform with a 600-kilometre orbit launched once a year between the launching of nuclear-powered rorsat pairs.

Early Warning Satellites
These are looked at in detail in the section on nuclear force command and control in Chapter 6.

Communications Satellites
Communications form the nervous system of a military force and the potential of military 'comsats' was immediately obvious. President Eisenhower used the United States' first communications satellite, 'Project Score', to broadcast a message for Christmas 1958 but

the subsequent development of military comsats has not been so pacific in nature. The US Army's 'Courier', launched in 1960, operated for a mere 18 days, and the US Air Force's controversial West Ford project in 1961 involved spreading a huge cloud of copper needles in space as a reflective screen from which to bounce radio messages. With more powerful boosters available by 1966, the US successfully orbited seven satellites in the Initial Defense Satellite Communications System (IDSCS), completing the network of 26 satellites in 1968. Each satellite was put into near synchronous orbit at 33 915 kilometres staying in view of an equatorial receiving station for $4\frac{1}{2}$ days. The system was used during the Viet Nam war for trans-Pacific communication but each satellite had only one SHF channel capable of relaying ten kBits of voice data (the latest Block III DSCS series has a 32-MBit capacity or 1300 two-way conversations simultaneously).

DSCS Phase II comprises 16 satellites with an operational life stretching into the 1990s. The systems have steerable narrow beam antennae which allow small ground stations to receive transmissions, so enabling tactical usage of the system. The DCSC III series began operations in 1983 with the first launched into geosynchronous orbit on October 30 by Titan 34D/IUS from Cape Canaveral. The system is designed to be resistant to jamming, is able to provide secure strategic and tactical voice and data transmission, military command and control, and ground mobile communication. Of its 500 possible subscribers roughly 80 will be for the 'Wimex' or the US DoD's World Wide Minimum Command and Control System (WWMCCS), 50 for the US Navy and 300 for the US Air Force, Army and Marine Corps, taking over from submarine, cable or UHF radio links, a large proportion of it at present leased from commercial operators. Other subscribers are the State Department's Diplomatic Telecommunications Service, the White House Communications Agency, NATO and the United Kingdom.

While the DSCS system is primarily concerned with the transmission of material from major facility to major facility, the FLSATCOM/AFSATCOM network is designed to communicate with military units, including SIOP-dedicated nuclear armed forces, in the field, at sea or airborne. (SIOP is the US Single Integrated Operational Plan for nuclear war fighting — see chapter 3.) The four operational (and one spare) satellites of the FLSATCOM network were launched into geosynchronous orbit over a three-year period from Cape Canaveral. Each provides nine 25 kHz channels for fleet relay, a fleet

Left: *FLSATCOM satellite. Four were launched into geosynchronous orbit with one spare to create a global relay network for US armed forces communications*

Below: *Ford Aerospace third generation NATO III communications satellite uses a wide beam antenna for coverage from the US east coast to the eastern Mediterranean and a narrow beam antenna for European use*

Right: *One of the Phase II DFCS satellites, part of the United States' primary comsat network. Steerable narrow beam antennae allow small ground stations to receive transmissions*

A transportable earth station can transmit or receive messages via orbiting comsats to almost any point on the globe

broadcast channel, a 500 kHz wide-band channel for general US DoD users, and 12 dedicated channels assigned to AFSATCOM, or Air Force Satellite Communications, which permit satellite communications with strategic Air Command's EC-135 flying command posts, B-52 and FB-111A bombers, Minuteman launch centres and SAC headquarters. AFSATCOM transponders are also carried by other 'host satellites'.

These include the 'Satellite Data System' (SDS) launched periodically from 1971 and put into highly elliptical orbits. Their function is obscure, although officially described (US Air Force Research Test and Evaluation Budget Request Before Congress FY 1984) as:

'SDS provides one of the major host satellites supporting the AFSATCOM system. It provides critical two-way transpolar command and communications for our nuclear capable forces (where the other geostationary comsats cannot reach). SDS also supports a data communications network and the Satellite Test Center for command and control of our satellites.' It is assumed in fact that the SDS series relays data from KH11 and other digital transmission spy satellites.

FLSATCOM/AFSATCOM will be supplemented and replaced by MilStar or 'Military Strategic Tactical and Relay' by the late 1980s. MilStar reflects the emphasis on survivability in the age of the ASAT and will consist of at least four satellites, hardened against the effects of electromagnetic pulse (EMP) and directed energy weapons, placed in geostationary orbit over the Indian, East and West Pacific and Atlantic oceans. However, a number of spares will be placed much further out at 177 000 kilometres in 'super synchronous' orbits safe from direct ascent weapons or co-orbital ASATS, waiting to be called down to replace their counterparts knocked out of any space war front line.

NATO also has its own dedicated comsats. The first two were launched in 1970 and 1971 covering the North Atlantic and Europe from the US east coast as far as Turkey. There are currently four NATO-3 series satellites with the option of a fifth to extend service life. After a rather undistinguished early history, the British 'Skynet' programme is still active with a double launching (Skynet 4A and 4B) by Shuttle due in 1985. Previous launches were by Thor-Delta from Cape Canaveral. The French Telecom series due for launch by Ariane in 1985 will feed into the 'Syracuse' system which links military installations and mobile receivers.

Soviet Comsats
Soviet satellite communications, like so much else in the Soviet system, show an overlap between civil and military needs. The first of the Molniya (lightning) series was launched in 1965 with a highly elliptical orbit chosen to give the longest possible coverage of Soviet national territory each day. The first Soviet synchronous satellite was launched in 1974 and there has been a slow shift to increased use of technique, each equipped with multiple broad-band channel repeaters which may point to the relay of digital imagery from other satellites.

Direct tactical communications between ground and naval forces are achieved by a unique system. These small 'storage dump' satellites are launched eight at a time from a single C-1 booster from Plesetsk into 1500-kilometre orbits. A minimum of 24 of these one-metre diameter spheres are needed to provide global coverage providing realtime radio communications over the USSR and Eastern Europe and 'delayed' messages worldwide. Commands are radioed up to the satellite, recorded, then played back to the relevant recipient when coverage is attained. A larger satellite in the Cosmos series is believed to use the same technique and it has been suggested that this may have been used for covert activities, receiving messages from clandestine sources.

The large number of Soviet tactical Comsats (up to 48 at any one time) and the long orbital life of them and their rocket stages means their orbits are becoming cluttered with defunct hardware — enough, one day, to invite the attention of an orbital dust cart in the shape of a Soviet shuttle.

Navigation
The development of nuclear weapons and nuclear strategy has been profoundly affected by developments in space. The accuracy of today's intercontinental, submarine-launched and theatre weapons would be impossible without the geophysical surveys conducted from space, the creation of digitalised computer maps, the position-fixing of ballistic missile submarines, and the collection of information on gravity, the behaviour of ocean currents, and so on by space-based experiments.

The latest US navsat programme is called 'Navstar'. The key to Navstar is extremely accurate timekeeping based on three rubidium automatic clocks, built into each satellite and accurate to within one second in thirty-six thousand years. Eight Navstar satellites had been launched by 1983 and a long-term contract was issued in 1984 for 28 follow-ons, each with an operational life of up to ten years. Navstar users, ranging from ballistic missiles to infantry in the field, are equipped with computerised receivers which transform the space-originated grids of time and range signals into a navigational fix, accurate to within 16 metres.

There has been Congressional speculation that the Soviet equivalent, 'Glonass', might be programmed to patch into the Navstar network and that Soviet military forces, with access to the right receivers and codes, could also tap into Navstar navigational data. Glonass uses a similar technology to the US system with up to twelve satellites at 20 000-kilometre orbits.

Weather
Weather is perhaps the area where military and civil space use has most overlapped. The primary function of military weather reconnaissance is in fact to support photo reconnaissance activity which would be baffled by cloud cover. The US military began flying weather satellites in 1965 and the current US Block 5D weather satellite, first flown in the late 1970s, is equipped with daylight and infra-red cameras to monitor cloudcover, as well as instruments to take pressure, water vapour and temperature readings, transmitting data back to ground terminals at either the US Air Force's Global Weather Center or the Civil National Oceanic and Atmospheric Administration (NOAA), with which the DSMP (Defense Meteorological Satellite Program) is shared.

Soviet military and civil weather reconnaissance also overlaps. Two or three Meteor 2s operate in an 890-kilometre, 81-degree orbit using scanning radiometers able to monitor cloud cover at night, unlike the daylight-only TV cameras of earlier satellites in the series. Pictures are provided at four-hour intervals to ground stations within the Soviet Union.

Star Wars

In April 1983 President Reagan went public with, in· his words, 'a vision of the future which offers hope'. The new vision, details of which were delivered almost casually, seemed set to overturn the fundamental tenets on which the doctrines of nuclear deterrence had been so precariously built. The President called for the threat of retaliation to be abandoned in favour of a defensive strategy offering the notion of 'assured survival'. The political moment for such a pronouncement had come because of the deadlock in superpower arms control diplomacy, the Reagan administration's determination to wrest military superiority back from the Soviets and because the technology of directed weapons seemed sufficiently mature to make the proposal seem more than just science fiction. There are important shades of opinion as to just what a space-based defence force is designed to defend. As it stands in the short term, directed energy weapons in space would be ASAT systems only. Next would be a space-based ABM system which might protect purely military targets such as ICBM missile silos from attack by rival ICBMs, so underpinning assured retaliation rather than the assured survival which continental defence would require.

Such a goal would require a multi-layered defence which would begin with orbiting 'battlestars' and end with ground-based terminal defence. One study proposes eighteen battlestars, placed in 1750-kilometre polar orbits in three rings, armed with chemical lasers. The system would have a maximum of 300 seconds to destroy up to 3000 attacking missiles, 300 seconds being the time between the missile leaving the atmosphere and the burnout of the final stage before the multiple warheads separate. The study concludes that two or three shuttle payloads would be enough to place each battlestar in orbit, the first mission to take up the laser itself, its battle management computers and target acquisition systems, then subsequent flights to carry up fuel tanks for up to 19 minutes of laser firings.

Missiles theoretically could be 'hardened' to resist the effects of laser illumination by covering them in ablative heat-absorbing material, polishing their surfaces into highly reflective mirror coatings or spinning them so that the surface area is constantly sweeping round so laser energy cannot be concentrated on one spot.

The US Defense Advanced Projects Research Agency (DARPA) is managing three key experimental programmes in the joint US Air Force/DARPA space-based laser effort. The so-called Space Laser Triad covers the programme 'Alpha', to develop a ground-based three-megawatt hydrogen fluoride continuous wave laser. By adding generator modules it is planned to generate extremely high power beams of up to ten megawatts. The second element is 'Lode' or Large Optics Demonstration Experiment which is a ground-based demonstration of critical beam control technology dependent, initially, on a four-metre diameter primary mirror manufactured to supercritical tolerances. 'Talon Gold' is the part of the experimental programme concerned with the all-important tracking and pointing. The aim is to be able to track a target 1500 kilometres away, with an accuracy of 0·2 microradian. Using a low powered laser, Talon Gold will assess the problems of basing a high powered laser in space and will be tested against high altitude aircraft and space targets.

According to recent DARPA congressional testimony there is a further Strategic Technology Program Element that supports both the near term Triad experiments and further term short wavelength laser systems. 'Its major emphasis is to build upon the Triad technologies and attempt, at a component level, to provide a basis for advanced systems both at infra-red and shorter wavelengths. The scope of our current short wavelength laser program includes: advanced short wavelength laser devices including free electron and exciter, precision pointing capability for short wavelength lasers, and fire-control technologies required for engaging various targets.'

One potentially important high technology space programme should be examined which is not related to the Star Wars issue. If space-based directed energy weapons do indeed end the invincibility of ICBMs, offensive weapon systems that are 'air breathing', that is stay within the atmosphere, such as manned aircraft and cruise missiles may find their time comes round again. The US Air Force's Teal Ruby programme plans to demonstrate the feasibility of tracking low-altitude air targets from a space-based platform using 'staring mosaic' radar, picking up indications of moving targets against the background clutter of the earth itself. Tests are due for 1986, lasting one year.

While 'Star Wars' research is primarily directed to investigate the potential of directed energy weapons in space, the US Army's anti-ballistic missile research programme has continued with less ambitious concepts. This is an artist's impression of a homing overlay ABM which is designed to deploy a mesh in the path of an incoming hostile missile

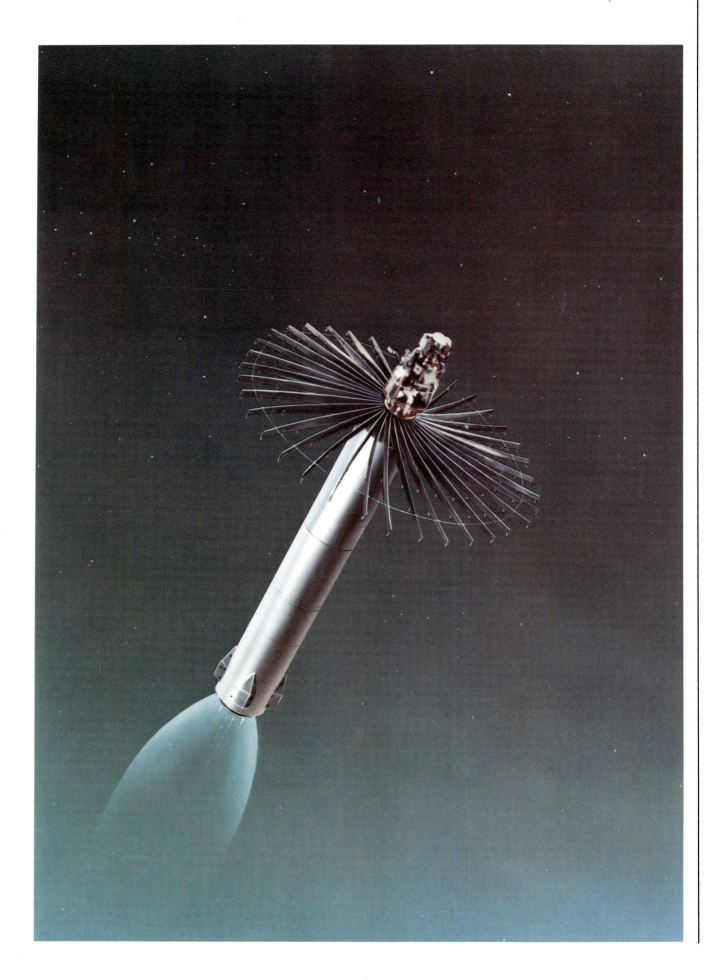

ASATS

The United States in fact had a direct ascent low latitude anti-satellite capability from 1963–75, using experimental anti-ballistic missile missiles such as Army Nike-Zeus and US Air Force Thors, both with nuclear warheads. The Soviet Union also experimented with direct ascent nuclear-armed ASAT missiles based on their first generation ABMs but in the end followed another route, that of the co-orbital hunter-killer ASAT. The first such US programme, SAINT (Satellite Interceptor Inspection and Negation), ran from 1960–62 at the height of concern over possible nuclear weapons actually being placed in orbit. It was a programme, like the first generation reconsats of the Discoverer series, based on the Agena upper stage for a co-orbital system which would be able to 'inspect' suspicious objects in orbit but was not in itself armed. The Soviets began tests of a co-orbital hunter-killer, which would close on its victims then self destruct lethally, in 1967. Tests continued fitfully through the 1970s and were discontinued during the abortive US-Soviet ASAT limitation talks of 1978–79. Progress with the Shuttle did not help as the Soviets claimed its ability to retrieve satellites in orbit made it an ASAT system itself.

Soviet tests were resumed in 1980 using a new 'pop-up' technique enabling an interception to be made half an hour from the ASAT's launch. They would however take over six hours to reach the critical systems which are placed in geosynchronous orbit and there is no evidence yet of an ability to close in on manoeuvring targets. Nevertheless, using the measure that manoeuvring within one kilometre of a target satellite is success, 13 out of 20 have fulfilled their mission in the orbital altitudes at which US Transit, SSBN navigation, Elint, weather and some photo reconnaissance satellites operate.

Rumours have long persisted of a Soviet ability to destroy satellites with direct ascent missiles or blind them with ground-based lasers. The US DoD has reported to Congress that the Soviet Union would be able to launch the first prototype space-based laser by the late 1980s, both rumours and official reports serving to loosen the political pursestrings on US directed energy and space weapon programmes.

The US meanwhile has regained an ASAT capacity with the F-15 Eagle aircraft and Vought ASAT missile combination, first test firing of which (not against a space target) took place in January 1984. The F-15 ASAT was originally selected as a relatively cheap and quick way of getting back in the anti-satellite business but Congress has been warned that it eventually cost 'in the tens of billions' of dollars while Soviet propoganda has been vilifying it every step of the way.

The F-15 system is a two-stage rocket launched at the fighter aircraft's extreme alti-

tude, either in a zoom climb or flying straight and level. The 'kill mechanism' is the Vought Miniature Vehicle which is intended to destroy its target by direct high velocity impact. The seeker head contains a cryogenically-cooled infra-red sensor with eight telescopes revolving at high speed which will pick up on the target against the cold background of space. A ring of 56 miniature one-shot rocket motors obey the on-board guidance commands to steer the system towards the heat source. It is not yet effective against manoeuvring systems (including therefore rival Soviet ASATs) and only functions in comparatively low orbit.

Right: *Loading a development ASAT on an F-15.* **Below:** *The F-15/ASAT combination, if it is put into service, will give the USAF a globally deployable, very quick reaction anti-satellite system but only against targets in relatively low orbit*

8 WAR
AT SEA

Even in the age of the nuclear-powered, ballistic missile firing submarine, the role of naval forces has remained the traditional one — to win *sea control* and, having won it, to exercise *seapower* by bringing aid and comfort to one's friends and disadvantage to one's foes. Sea control is no longer decided by a duel between ships but by a complex, interlocking battle to be waged above, on and under the sea, fought in an arena stretching from ocean reconnaissance satellites in orbit to networks of sensors deep in the ocean. The 'traditional' warship has not only survived but has become more significant than ever

because it remains the best if not the only means of effecting seapower once sea control has been won. The submarine is at once the most potent challenger to the retention of sea control and an instrument of mixed effectiveness in its defence. The nuclear-powered attack submarine HMS *Conqueror* for example, that sank the Argentinian cruiser *General Belgrano* in the South Atlantic war of 1982, was effective in enforcing an all-out blockade but was a blunt instrument of diplomacy — the only way it could reveal its presence was by making an attack.

The Falklands war was a worked example

While aircraft and submarines are potent instruments of sea warfare they are uncertain in the exercise of sea power itself.
Right: *French Navy Atlantique NG armed with homing torpedoes and air-launched Exocet*
Below: *HMS Turbulent, Royal Navy nuclear-powered attack submarine armed with Sub-Harpoon*

illustrating the concepts of the winning of sea control and the exercise of seapower. In fact it was hardly fought between warships at all, apart from the *Belgrano* sinking. Land-based air forces attempted to destroy British warships which were striving to exercise seapower without having won sea control by clearing the enemy from the skies. The sinking of HMS *Sheffield* by an air-launched Exocet highlighted the guided anti-ship missile threat however, but many more Royal Navy warships might have been lost had Argentinian 'iron bombs' been correctly fuzed for low level release (where the Skyhawks and Mirages were forced to operate, brought down by the comparative effectiveness of British shipborne medium-range surface-to-air missiles). Once the Argentinian air threat had been contained, although never completely, the Task Force was able to close on the contended islands, provide shore bombardment by naval guns and carrier aircraft and land troops in a classic expression of 'power projection'.

Submarines cannot project power by transporting a task force nor 'police' a blockade in anything but the highest intensity warfare. Submarines as yet cannot affect the battle for air superiority or contribute to fleet air defence although autonomous vertical launch missiles are under development which might allow them to do so. Yet the submarine is the deadly enemy of the surface ship, able to dispatch an aircraft carrier not with torpedoes, but with a salvo of cruise missiles launched from over the horizon, or to wreak havoc with a vital replenishment convoy. The fleet ballistic submarine has enough nuclear destructive power aboard to rip out the heart of an industrialised country while the proliferation of cruise missiles in conventional and nuclear land-attack variants is set to give deep attack capability to submarines configured to make war merely upon the oceans. The composite seapower of today and the technology that supports it, is therefore tilted very much towards the submarine — either making it more effective or dedicated to hunting it down. An important aspect of this process is that, in certain applications, the most effective adversary of the submarine is another submarine.

Again with reference to the South Atlantic fighting, the Royal Navy surface warships judged most effective were newer designs intended for the anti-submarine role on NATO's northern maritime flank (the so-called Greenland Iceland UK Gap (GIUK) such as the *Invincible* support carrier and the Type 22 anti-submarine frigate. These had enough flexibility and appropriate weapons systems to survive and win in conditions for which they were not designed. From the 1960s onwards the Royal Navy has been configured to operate as a component of NATO in an area (the North Atlantic) and against an enemy of critical significance — the Soviet Navy and in particular Soviet submarines.

The great anti-submarine campaign of the Second World War against German U-Boats in the Atlantic was decided as much by technology as by operations. At the end however, although operationally defeated, the German Navy's U-boat arm was on the technological offensive with the introduction of the first of a new type of fast and quiet boat, the type XXI, capable of outrunning Allied surface escorts, evading sonar detection and attacking with first generation 'smart' torpedoes. Wartime Soviet submarine operations in the Baltic were not significant but the lessons of the Battle of the Atlantic, how it was lost and how it was won, were eagerly examined, as were the prototypes of the Kriegsmarine's last weapons in the battle. The submarine was

judged the ideal instrument with which to challenge the West, and the construction of a formidable force has been undertaken with complete continuity of purpose. In the first phase the Soviet emphasis was defensive, with submarines designed as 'carrier-killers' to attack the US Navy's aircraft carriers; at the time US carriers were significant instruments of strategic nuclear attack on the Soviet Union. In fact the Soviet Navy got a ballistic missile to sea in a submarine first with the comparatively crude SS-N-4 of 1955, but when the US Navy began to deploy the much more sophisticated Polaris submarine sea-launched ballistic missile (SLBM) in strength in the early 1960s, the Soviet emphasis shifted to anti-submarine operations. With the advent of a large scale Soviet SSBN force with mass production of the *Yankee* class SSBN this continued, the assumption being made early on that the most effective way to stalk and destroy an enemy submarine was to use another submarine.

The first nuclear-powered submarines, the *November* class laid down in 1958, were designed from the outset as anti-submarine warfare (ASW) hunter-killers. When the USA deployed longer range, submarine-based ballistic missiles the task of searching the

Left: *To survive in the age of the surface-skimming cruise missile, composite seapower requires a wide range of specially configured warships linked by an electronic network of sensors and communications. While a helicopter provides ASW cover, a destroyer provides close escort for a US super carrier, itself the centre of a Task Group with assault ships left*

Right: *Victor III class submarine of the Soviet Navy*

Atlantic while NATO looked on was beyond the powers of Soviet surface ASW units. The solution was to build more submarines with range and endurance to wait near the enemy's home ports and stalk their prey to the deep ocean patrol areas. The *Victor* class was designed for this role and was followed in 1968 by the *Charlie* class. These were armed with cruise missiles that flew through the air to their target after underwater launch: the US Navy did not catch up with this kind of capability for another ten years.

In 1972 the pendulum began to swing the other way when the *Delta* I class SSBN became operational. These were armed with SS-N-8 missiles that had a range commanding targets in North America. Now it would be Western ASW forces that would have to contest an ever increasing Soviet anti-submarine screen, both on and sub-surface. The Deltas continued to be commissioned throughout the 1970s, the last *Delta III* class mounting sixteen S-N-8 SLBMs with a range of over 7000 kilometres and MIRV (multiple independently targetable re-entry vehicle) warheads. In 1979 the existence of a new missile, the solid fuel SS-NX-20 with an 8000-kilometre range, was publicised in the West and soon

afterwards a colossal launching platform was revealed — the *Typhoon* class, the largest submarine ever built, powered by two nuclear reactors and with a submerged displacement of 30 000 tons.

The investment in attack submarines continued during the 1970s, the cruise missile firing *Charlies*, and the *Victor* class were developed through improved models while the boats of the *Alfa* class with titanium alloy hulls began to appear with a reported diving capacity (over 900 metres) and a submerged speed (42 knots) which provided ASW problems of an entirely new order. The conventional attack submarine building programme has also kept pace, the relatively large 3000-ton *Tango* class replacing the *Foxtrot*. *Tangos* are intended to cover the large shallow water maritime approaches to the Soviet Union where nuclear-powered equivalents would be less operationally efficient and where the silent running or dead stop capacities of diesel-electrics can be best used as ASW listening platforms. (A nuclear submarine can never be entirely silent as it has to pump water constantly to cool its reactor core.)

The Soviet Navy, like NATO navies, has

followed two distinct strategies in developing its weapons technology and structuring its ASW forces — that of screening and hunter-killer. The classic expression of the screening tactic is the convoy, another is the creation of sanctuaries in which SLBM-armed submarines can operate, immune from direct attack. The hunter-killer strategy involves just that, seeking out the attacking enemy sub-surface units as rapidly and effectively as possible.

The operation of sensor networks, such as the US Navy's SOSUS (Sound Surveillance System), of fixed hydrophone arrays plus ocean reconnaissance satellites and land-based maritime air operations make the hunter-killer strategy viable in certain areas, if not turning the oceans transparent at least highlighting areas of interest and stacking up the odds against the hunted. ASW surface units designed for convoy escort need not be as sophisticated and expensive as those designed for offensive hunter-killer operations in contested waters — at least in theory. One problem however is the great size and complexity of modern long-range active sonars which demand comparatively large vessels to accommodate them and their associated electronics. A US Navy *Spruance* class destroyer for example, designed for anti-submarine warfare and with a big bow-mounted sonar, is as big as a wartime cruiser.

ASW Sensors

The dominant technological thrust in anti-submarine warfare has been the development of sensors and weapons of ever greater range, at least that is at the rate that offensive submarine weapons have developed from short-range unguided torpedoes to under-water-launched cruise missiles attacking at long range from over the horizon, so the need to get a blow in before the predator can strike and to have weapons with the range, the speed and the accuracy to do the job becomes more and more urgent.

First the predator must be discovered. A submerged submarine may be cloaked by the ocean but it is still a large metallic object that reflects sound waves propagated through the water. Secondly it makes a noise itself and leaves certain other traces of its passing. Sonar, the word derived from sound naviga-tion and ranging, is therefore the primary ASW sensor, working by emitting a beam of high intensity sound into seawater and inter-preting the echoes. Again, because subma-rine-launched cruise missiles can be launched from beyond the range of any target's ship-borne sonar, successful ASW screening means taking the sensor out to the likely area where the submarine might be. Fixed arrays of hydrophones such as the US Navy's SOSUS

system narrow the search area but taking the sensor to the target area means using fixed wing aircraft and helicopters to sow patterns of sonobuoys or using dipping sonars to sweep suspect areas. Since 1945 sonar power and ranges have increased, accompanied by equivalent advances in computerised signal processing and interpretation of the results but there are physical limits imposed both by the size of modern long-range active sonars and the physical properties of the oceans.

One technique, called 'bottom bounce propagation' and introduced in the 1950s uses sonar pulses bounced off the ocean floor to get the extra range. However the sea has its own highly complex dynamics of pressure, temperatures and salinity which affect the velocity and direction of travel of sound waves. For example, over large areas of the world's oceans a layer of relatively stable temperature extends downwards until it meets a 'thermocline' delineating the bound-ary between it and a deeper layer of greater pressure and different temperature. In the North Atlantic for instance, persistent storm action churns the wave tops to create a sur-face layer of nearly uniform temperature up to 600 feet deep. In the Mediterranean in summer the layer is very shallow. The impor-tant point is that sonar returns will tend to bounce off the thermocline, in effect are trap-ped within it so a submarine below the reflec-tive thermocline will be hidden from sonar contact.

A steeply angled beam, however, can be made to pierce the layer and bounce up and out to strike the fugitive submarine from below. The second key technique is con-vergence zone operation which uses the thermocline to bounce sound waves back up and out to the surface where in turn they are bounced down and forward again reaching out to 100 kilometres and more. Detection by this technique is limited to the area of the zone itself, a circular area which moves rela-tive to the movement of the ship generating it. Both bottom bounce and convergence zone techniques function best in deep water so navies with commitments in shallow waters have emphasised another solution to the layer problem using variable depth sonar (VDS) in which the transducer is streamed beneath and behind the warship under the thermocline.

Another very important technique is pas-sive sonar in which instead of actively 'pinging' and listening to the returns, the sounds emitted by a vessel are the source of target acquisition and characterisation. Pas-sive sonar was for a long time the preserve of the submarine, the range and bearing of a surface target for example being gleaned

Sonar range can be extended by using lower frequencies at greater power and by bouncing emissions off the sea bed or the 'thermocline', a reflective layer where two volumes of water of different pressure and temperature meet. 'Convergence Zones' are created where the reflected sound waves are bounced up and out onto the surface, then down and out again but both techniques are limited to deep water

The means by which submarines can be detected is diverse but long range systems depend in part on sonar: sound navigation and ranging, by which the target is detected either by reflecting emissions from a sonar source (active sonar) or by detection of their own sound (passive sonar): An ASW can use hull-mounted or variable-depth sonar to get below the screening thermocline. Helicopters can use dipping sonar to make localised searches. Networks of passive sea bed sensors can direct aircraft to search areas to make localised searches using parachute-dropped sonobuoys. Submarines and surface warships stream towed array passive sonars, remote from their own noise

SONAR PROPAGATION

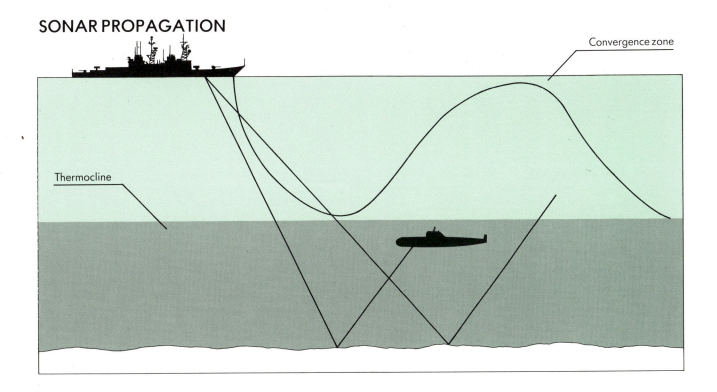

Convergence zone

Thermocline

ASW SENSORS

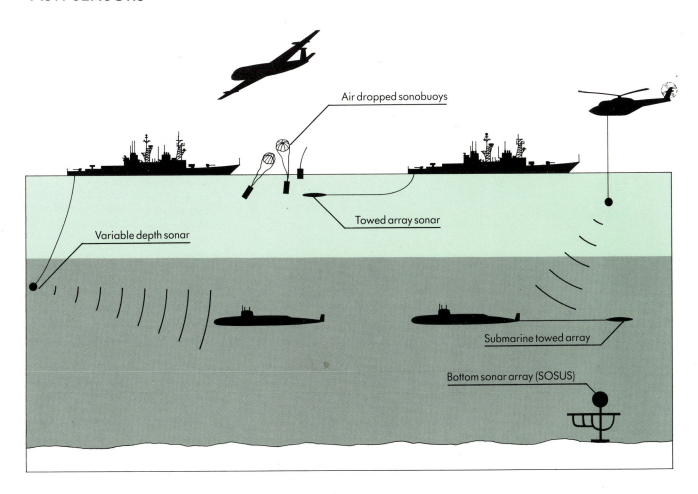

Air dropped sonobuoys

Towed array sonar

Variable depth sonar

Submarine towed array

Bottom sonar array (SOSUS)

from the sound of its engines and propeller which in turn gave further clues to its identity — a high-powered warship or a slower moving merchantman. In the last decade an important development has been the introduction of towed array sonar on submarines, the listening devices being streamed behind the submarine, remote from its own noise. The US Navy's fleet of nuclear-powered attack submarines is fitted with the AN/BQQ-5 towed array sonar which streams a hydrophone array 800 metres aft of the boat with a speed penalty of only 0·5 knot and no serious affect on submerged handling. In the Falklands campaign HMS *Conqueror* first picked up the *General Belgrano* and her escort group using Type 2024 towed array sonar.

High-speed towed arrays are also being applied to surface ASW units. Remote from the warship's own noise they are effective at ranges of up to 70 kilometres and a screening force of towed array-equipped escorts could force submarines attacking from the flanks to reveal themselves by their own need to move at high speed to attack so making much more noise.

Towed array technology forms a significant

proportion of the US Navy's long term plans to keep its global underwater surveillance abreast of expanding capabilities and new types of submarine such as the exceptionally deep diving and fast *Alfa* class. While the fixed SOSUS network, originally conceived in the 1950s has been upgraded with advanced signal processing techniques and expanded, as system called SURTASS (Surveillance Towed Array Sensor System) is designed to make the overall system far more flexible and survivable. It does so by using small purpose-built warships to sweep designated areas with the long SURTASS arrays receiving and transmitting data, via satellite if necessary to shore stations where powerful computers will strive to decipher the subsea cacophony.

A further element is RDSS, the Rapidly Deployable Surveillance System using air-dropped, long-life, bottom-moored buoys

Above: *Lockheed S-3A Viking carrier-borne ASW aircraft. The tail extension houses a Magnetic Anomaly Detector able to detect submerged metallic objects at close range*

Left: *Cable drums aboard a French Navy destroyer for Thomson-CSF towed array sonar*

Right: *Royal Navy Westland Sea King about to immerse its Plessey Type 195 dipping sonar*

equipped with listening devices to chart submarine movements, relaying information to ASW aircraft.

The continued effectiveness of the SOSUS Network which concentrates very much on the North Atlantic allowed the US and other navies to develop tactical doctrines and pursue weapons based on the hunter-killer strand of ASW rather than the more passive close escort of convoys. This was possible because, for the time being at least, the position of relatively noisy Soviet submarines can be plotted on a near real time basis and offensive forces targeted against them with a chance of success. The weapon system ideally suited to exploit this situation was the land-based ASW aircraft such as the US Navy's P-3 Orion or the RAF's Nimrod M R 1 equipped with air-dropped sonobuoys to localise the search area, and magnetic anomaly detectors (MADs) to fix the target, and offensive weapons in the shape of homing torpedoes or nuclear depth bombs.

ASW Weapons

The principle submarine-to-submarine ASW weapon is the wire-guided torpedo. Target acquisition and mid-course guidance are handled by the submarine's own fire-control computer. This transmits guidance commands down trailing wires while the weapon's own short-range active sonar takes over in the terminal phase. The torpedo must of course be faster than the submarine which it is chasing, a fact which poses particular design problems when faced with the 40-knot plus submerged top speed of some Soviet submarines. The Mk 48 heavy torpedo for example, equipping all US Navy attack and fleet ballistic missile submarines has a speed of 55 knots and a range of almost 40 kilometres. A number of US Navy submarines also carry a system called Subroc, a guided missile launched underwater from forward torpedo tubes which follows a short underwater path, breaks surface and flies up to 56 kilometres before releasing the warhead, a nuclear depth bomb with a one kiloton yield and a lethal radius of up to eight kilometres. A nuclear-armed torpedo called Astor was developed as a last ditch self-defence weapon for submarines but it was credited with a kill probability of 2:0 — the target and the launch submarine. Soviet submarines are known to

Right: *Tigerfish, the Royal Navy's standard heavyweight wire-guided torpedo. Range is over 20 km*

Below: *Thomson-CSF Murene lightweight homing torpedo*

operate a similar system to Subroc, code-named SS-N-15, equipping boats of the *Papa, Alfa, Victor III* and *Tango* classes.

On present plans Subroc will be replaced in the US Navy by a system called ASW-SOW (anti-submarine stand-off weapon) which will carry a lightweight homing torpedo as an alternative payload to a nuclear depth bomb. ASW-SOW will also replace Asroc on US Navy surface escorts as the primary shipborne anti-submarine weapon, employing an operational profile very similar to the current weapon but with greater technical sophistication and a vertical launch capability. Asroc has been operational since 1961 and consists of a short-range missile (two to ten kilometres) carrying a nuclear depth bomb or a Mk 46 acoustic homing torpedo. The Mk 46's method of operation is typical of the type — immediately on entering the water it begins a descending helical search pattern, sweeping a 'lethal volume' within which its own autonomous terminal homing will operate. If it fails to acquire a target it will start again, being capable of multiple consecutive attacks. An improvement programme called Neartip is in hand for the Mk 46, significantly designed to restore its acquisition range (estimated at some 450 metres) in the face of Soviet sound-reduction technology and in particular the use of anechoic or sound-absorbing coatings on submarines. Asroc and the ASW-SOW system planned to replace it are ballistic missiles technically capable of all-weather operation. Other navies have developed small robotic aircraft to carry homing torpedoes out to the likely target area; they have longer range but are bulkier and less all-weather capable. Typical systems are the French Malafon, the Australian Ikara and the Soviet SS-N-14 Silex, all with guided torpedoes as the payload. A passive homing torpedo however may not be able to home on a diesel-electric submarine lying silent on the sea bed and an active homer might not pick it out from the background. In modern ASW firepower, therefore, there is still room for the old mortar-fired depth bomb of the British 1950's vintage Limbo type.

The most effective way of taking the sensor

Above: *Air-launched sea-skimming anti-ship missiles showed their devastating impact in the Falklands War. Above: An AM 39 Exocet launched by a French Air Force Mirage F1. In the Gulf war anti-ship missiles launched by helicopter have also proved effective*

Left: *The SH-60B Seahawk is the US Navy's latest shipborne ASW helicopter. It can also act as an 'anti-ship surveillance and targeting' platform providing target acquisition data and mid-course guidance for ship-launched missiles. The Seahawk is shown here teamed with an Oliver Hazard Perry-class escort armed with Standard and Harpoon surface-to-surface missiles*

Exocet MM40 configured as a mobile coast defence battery. A missile launched from an improvised mounting struck the destroyer HMS Glamorgan during the Falklands fighting

and the weapon system to the submarine is by shipborne helicopter which after thirty years of development has evolved into one of the most complex pieces of military technology. The third generation US Navy Light Airborne Multi-Purpose System (LAMPS) in effect functions as a flying component of the ship, netted into its computer and communications power at the same time extending its anti-submarine reach of several hundred kilometres. A LAMPS III detachment numbers 15 people, three as crew in the SH-60B Seahawk helicopter, the remainder on the parent warship. There the air tactical control officer has command of the mission and indeed can operate some of the helicopter's equipment directly such as deploying sonobuoys. The acoustic signals picked up by the pattern of sonobuoys are relayed to the helicopter and thence to the ship for analysis in the combat information centre. If a target is located, the mission commander orders the helicopter to confirm contact by deploying active or passive directional sonobuoys or by trailing a MAD unit. When directed, attacks can be made with Mk 46 homing torpedoes.

The Seahawk can also operate as a platform for anti-ship surveillance and targeting (ASST) providing target information and midcourse guidance for shipborne anti-surface or anti-submarine weapons. In fact helicopters are considered important platforms themselves for anti-ship missiles and have proved effective in this role firing Exocets in the Gulf war and Royal Navy Lynxes Firing Sea Skua missiles against small surface targets in the South Atlantic fighting.

Anti-ship Missiles

The destruction of HMS *Sheffield* by an air-launched Exocet emphasised the vulnerability of surface warships in the age of missile warfare. Exocet is typical of the sea-skimming missiles developed from the late 1960s onwards which can be launched from a wide range of platforms including fast patrol boats, high performance aircraft, helicopters and submarines. Indeed it is the technology of the submarine-launched anti-shipping missile, its reach and its 'single shot kill probability' which make so urgent the kind of countermeasures outlined above. An analogy can be made with the missile launched by an aircraft at stand-off range, that is out of reach of the target's own defences and a submarine stalking its prey using stealth for protection. The defence priorities are the same — find the launch platform and destroy it before it can fire. If that fails, be prepared to destroy the weapon launched at you or baffle it with electronic countermeasures. To do that, the technology of the threat must be understood.

The Exocet is a very useful working example. In its ship-launched version the target co-ordinates are imparted to its inertial guidance system by the ship's fire-control system. On launch the missile flies towards that point, its on-board computer remembering where it was launched from and where it was told to go, making it in the jargon a true 'fire-and-forget' system. In mid-flight the missile descends to a height a few metres above the wavetops, using a down looking radar altimeter to maintain height and the radar clutter of the wavetops to hide from the target's defensive radar systems. In the last stage of the flight the missile's active homing head switches on, bringing the missile electronically live and therefore visible to the target's electronic support measures equipment but with only a few seconds of the flight now left. The terminal seeker directs the missile to home in on the biggest source of radar returns — the target warship. The air-launched version functions in exactly the same way except that the target co-ordinates are imparted by the launch aircraft's surface search radar, and it does not need a booster as the aircraft supplies the launch speed. A submarine-launched version has been devel-

oped which is all but identical to the air-launched version, using a pop-out capsule for underwater launch from torpedo tubes.

The Soviet Navy pioneered surface-to-surface anti-ship missiles and has put several generations into service. The latest is the SS-N-19 which has been identified as a vertically-launched system deployed both on the nuclear powered battlecruiser *Kirov* and the very large cruise missile firing submarine codenamed *Oscar*. NATO analysts credit the missile with a speed of Mach 2·5 and a range of no less 500 kilometres suggesting that aircraft or satellites would be used for mid-course guidance with autonomous terminal

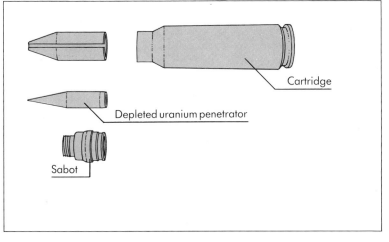

Cartridge

Depleted uranium penetrator

Sabot

VULCAN-PHALANX CIWS

The last ditch answer to the threat of the surface skimming anti-ship missile is a close in weapon system (CIWS) designed to literally put a radar directed wall of metal in the path of an incoming missile in the few seconds that might be left. After the Falklands campaign US-built Vulcan Phalanx systems were fitted to major Royal Navy surface units

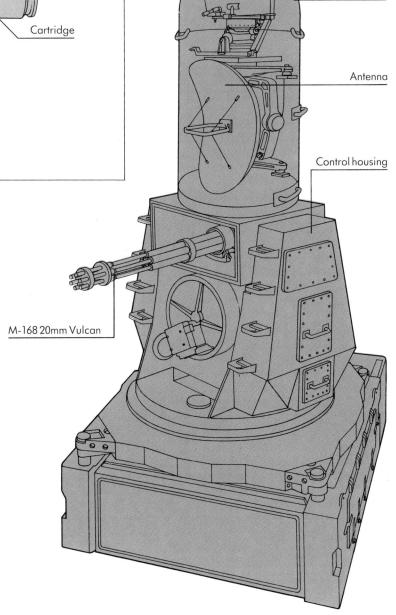

Radome

Antenna

Control housing

M-168 20mm Vulcan

Above: *Standard SM-2 test launch from the trials ship USS* Norton Sound. *The Standard is a dual-purpose surface-to-air or surface-to-surface missile*

Left: *Underwater launch of sub-Harpoon. Range is over 90 km and the system equips both US and Royal Navy nuclear powered attack submarines*

homing. The US Navy caught up relatively late, not getting the Harpoon anti-ship missile operational until 1977, since then however it has been widely deployed with applications across the US fleet from the reborn battleships of the *Iowa* class to patrol hydrofoils. It has also been developed for air launch from land based aircraft such as P-3 Orions, carrier aircraft such as the A-6 and from submarines. Sub-Harpoon has also been supplied to the Royal Navy though Exocet remains that service's principal surface-to-surface weapon.

Harpoon has a range of up to 90 kilometres. Capabilities of an entirely different order are the preserve of the Tomahawk sea-launched cruise missile (SLCM), with a range of 2500 kilometres in its land-attack version. Tomahawk is a system which blurs the distinction between tactical weapons for warfare against rival naval forces and a strategic bombardment weapon which potentially gives the destructive firepower of a nuclear ballistic missile submarine to the simplest of warships. The anti-ship version of Tomahawk has been engineered with either nuclear or conventional warheads. Range however is 450 kilometres and terminal guidance is via a modified version of the Harpoon's active radar system.

The threat of the surface-skimming anti-ship missile, air-surface or submarine-launched,

demands a huge technological effort in fleet defence, both in sensors to detect and identify targets at maximum range, and in defensive weapons systems to hit the hostile launch platform before the shot goes in or to shoot down the missile itself if all else fails. The US Navy with its seapower built around hugely expensive task groups is not surprisingly lavishly equipped with such systems and well rehearsed in the doctrines for their use. The solution is defence in depth with three distinct zones of operation and weapon effectiveness. Land-based maritime aircraft and attack submarines patrol the perimeter of the outer-zone on ASW duties, their operations co-ordinated with the fixed sensor networks such as SOSUS outlined earlier. Meanwhile in the 'air envelope' fleet air defence fighters such as F-14A Tomcats armed with very long range Phoenix air-to-air missiles fly combat air patrols (CAPs) to screen the fleet from cruise missile armed bombers such as the Tu-26 Backfire or long-range Tu-20 Bears able to provide mid-course guidance for submarine-launched missiles. Carrier based airborne early warning aircraft such as the Grumman E-2B provide long-range target detection and direct the CAP defence to maximum effect.

In the middle zone surface warships provide a second ring of ASW protection using

TYPE 22 DESTROYER

Designed originally as a general purpose escort, the Type 22 design eventually emerged optimised for anti-submarine warfare capable of fulfilling the Royal Navy's obligations in the north Atlantic. Nevertheless it was as an air defence ship armed with Seawolf missiles that the class came into itself in the Falklands fighting. Two sets of gas turbines afford a top speed of over 30 knots.

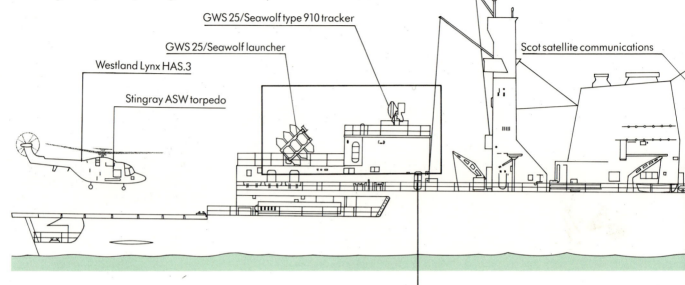

GWS 25/Seawolf type 910 tracker
GWS 25/Seawolf launcher
Westland Lynx HAS.3
Stingray ASW torpedo
Scot satellite communications

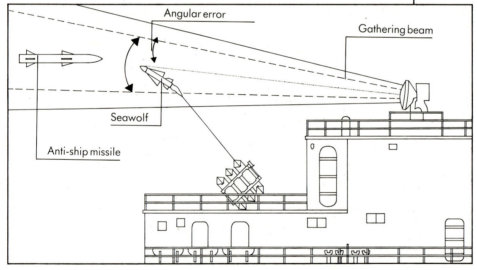

Angular error
Gathering beam
Seawolf
Anti-ship missile

Seawolf works by command guidance to line of sight, that is the Type 910 tracker radar tracks the course of both incoming target and missile, automatically generating correction commands and sending them to the missile

towed array sonars and directing LAMPS III helicopters to investigate contacts. Carrier-based SA-3 Vikings join in the search. In this zone long-range missile defence begins to cover the fleet.

In the inner zone ASW rockets and homing torpedoes are the last ditch defence against intruding submarines. In the air, point defences and electronic countermeasures are the last defence against air threats which by now will include supersonic cruise missiles and sea skimmers.

The technology of missile-based fleet air defence has developed in step with the doctrine of layered defence and the evolving nature of the threat. The critical problems are detection capacity, multiple target capability, reaction time, firepower, area coverage, reliability and resistance to electronic countermeasures. The US Navy's solution is called Aegis, a technologically hugely ambitious programme twenty years in development, to provide a leakproof umbrella for carrier battle groups. The heart of Aegis is the AN/SPY-1A phased array radar capable of the simultaneous detection and tracking of multiple targets and linked to four powerful computers which co-ordinate the targeting and launch of extended range SM-2 Standard missiles while the fire-control system and its

Far right: USS Ticonderoga, *lead ship of the Aegis-equipped class of warships designed to provide highly capable fleet air defence for US Navy battle groups. The planar antennae for the phased array radar system are clearly visible*

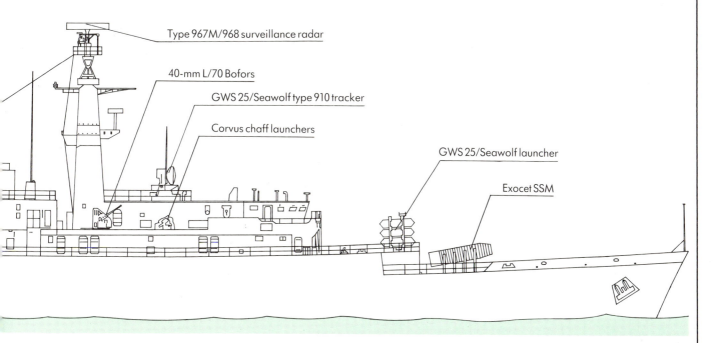

Type 967M/968 surveillance radar

40-mm L/70 Bofors

GWS 25/Seawolf type 910 tracker

Corvus chaff launchers

GWS 25/Seawolf launcher

Exocet SSM

associated radar illuminates the target. The Standard missile uses semi-active guidance, that is it has a radar receiver in its nose able to pick up energy generated by the shipborne target illumination radar reflected by the target on which it homes in its terminal flight phase. The British point defence Seawolf missile in contrast uses command guidance, the ship's radar tracks both the target and the missile itself after launch, or the missiles is tracked optically via a TV camera, the fire-control system sending it signals via a data link to come into the line of sight to the target. Aegis combines aspects of both systems. The Standard missile has an autopilot which the Aegis fire control computer sets before firing, taking the missile to the target area while the system also provides some mid-course correction via a command guidance link, the missile receiving the signals via rear-facing antennae. The illuminating radar need operate only in the terminal phase thus increasing the target load capability while the energy-efficient path made possible by steering the missile to the likely position of the target on impact rather than following it on line of sight means the slant range to the target is effectively doubled. The first Aegis cruiser USS *Ticonderoga* joined the fleet in 1983 and a further 23 are planned to become operational by the early 1990s. Later Aegis ships will have vertical launch systems (VLS) which offer much more efficient use of shipboard space and all-weather operability. It is planned that US shipborne weapons should conform to a common module compatible with the Mk 41 vertical launch system now in a state of

advanced development.

The Standard SM-2 can engage targets at ranges over 50 kilometres. At the other end of the air defence envelope are the superfast reacting close-in weapons systems (CIWS) designed to provide last ditch defence. The US Vulcan-Phalanx is a radar-guided multiple cannon firing at a cyclical rate of 3000 rounds a minute. The actual projectiles are 20 mm rounds of exceptionally dense depleted uranium which are designed literally to put a wall of metal in the path of an incoming sea skimmer. Phalanx is widely deployed throughout the US Navy and the Soviets have a similar 30 mm Gatling type CIWS plus associated radar installed on major surface units.

An urgent lesson of the Falklands fighting was the desperate need for short-range firepower, troops and sailors blazing away with whatever was to hand to at least put off the aim of aircraft which had evaded the long- and medium-range missile screens. Destroyers like *Glamorgan* and *Exeter* had their seaboats replaced by twin rapid fire 30 mm cannon while US Vulcan Phalanx systems were expeditiously acquired from the USA for installation on the support carriers *Illustrious* and *Invincible*. The Seawolf GWS 25 point defence missile fitted to the destroyers *Broadsword* and *Brilliant* proved itself technically proficient and no Seawolf-equipped ship was lost but they came close to being overwhelmed by mass attacks, each ship having only a dozen missiles ready to fire while its line of sight/command-guidance system meant that it could not engage targets that were not approaching the ship on which the Seawolf was mounted. The two Type 22s in the Falklands had to place themselves between the carriers and the likely direction of an attack and when missiles came in parallel or away from the ships, the Seawolf point defence system was largely ineffective.

Mine Warfare

The first Royal Navy ship into Port Stanley was significantly a minesweeper — in fact a requisitioned trawler which proved effective in sweeping the relatively crude mines laid by the Argentinians because the kind of technol-

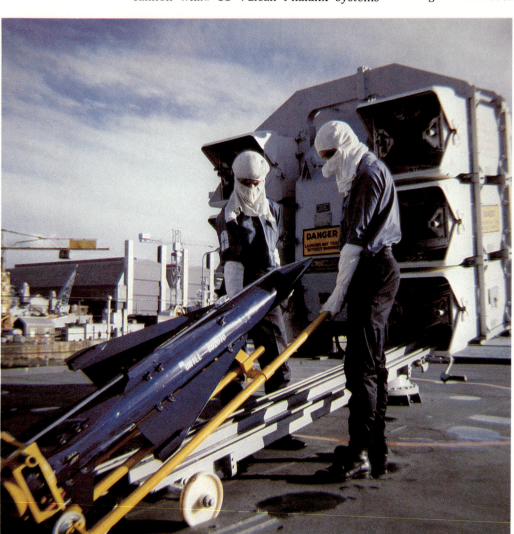

Left: *Royal Navy ratings load a Seawolf on HMS Broadsword's aft launcher. Manual reloading is an operational drawback but vertical launch systems are under development*

Right: *MBB Pinguin mine-hunting system, in essence a miniature robotic submarine equipped with its own sonar and cameras and capable of placing charges to neautralise bottom moored mines*

ogy that has made homing torpedoes and underwater warfare systems so effective also applies to the humble mine. Meanwhile, developments in sonar have opened up the technology of active 'mine-hunting', especially for mines laid on the sea bed. The simplest type in fact is the ground mine which can be sown in water up to 70 metres deep and which awaits the passage of a recognisable target overhead before rising to meet it. The older type of moored mine can be used at depths beyond the limits of the continental shelf, extending their effective target acquisition range by using acoustic, pressure or magnetic effects or a combination of fuzing techniques. The US Captor mine is a variation on the theme, a bottom-moored mine which can be layed at great depths which releases a Mk 46 anti-submarine homing torpedo once activated.

Mine countermeasure (MCM) vessels are akin to 'stealth' aircraft in that their signatures as presented to mine activation systems must be as low as possible. Hulls are therefore made of wood or glass fibre while extensive degaussing keeps remaining magnetic signatures low. Hulls are further designed to minimise pressure and noise while variable pitch propellers and general noise damping keep down acoustic signatures. Their roles divide into further specialities — the minesweeper

whose task is to cut the cables of bottom-moored mines or detonate ground mines harmlessly, the less traditional 'minehunter' which locates mines on the seabed via sonar then neutralises them with a remotely controlled submersible and the deep sweeper which, like the requisitioned trawlers used in the Falklands, is typically a deep-water stern trawler equipped to cut the cables of moored mines at depths close to the edge of the continental shelf. Aircraft are important platforms for minelaying and potentially for mine sweeping. The US Navy has led the technology of minesweeping via helicopter, deploying the large MH-53E Sea Stallion which tows a mine countermeasures sled through the water.

Weapons Systems and Weapons Platforms

The late twentieth century warship emphasises one design imperative above all others — that a warship as a weapons' platform is only as effective as the weapon systems which it is there to make mobile. A nuclear-powered aircraft carrier for example, for all the vast investment in hull and propulsion is still just a vast floating airfield surmounting an even bigger magazine packed with bombs, missiles, engineering space and aviation fuel. The carrier's power is invested in its aircraft

Above: *The massive RH-53D Sea Stallion helicopter is designed to tow a mine-countermeasure sled through the water*

Left: *Sowing a US Navy Mk6 Mod 5 bottom mine*

— it is as effective as they and the systems they carry are in strike and counter-air warfare. Aircraft carriers are exceptional, most modern surface warships are lineal descendants of the fast and high-powered warship of the destroyer type where size is a critical design factor. They suffer from a basic design problem that a small ship always needs more power per tonne to drive it through the water at a given speed than a large one because the proportion of waterline length in relation to

beam and draught directly effect speed. Power required per tonne is close to being a function of the ratio of speed to length — that is a 600-foot cruiser requires less power per tonne than a 400-foot destroyer to sustain the same speed.

Modern warships are not so much weight as volume critical — that is their efficiency in accommodating powerplants, fuel, electronics, tactical control centres, sonars, helicopter hangarage, crew accommodation, weapon systems and so on. At first sight a warship of the 'eighties might not appear to be armed at all, just a platform for mast mounted radars, a few cryptic radomes, a missile launcher or two, perhaps a single puny looking gun. The apparent sparseness belies the power of the weapon systems themselves, that single gun, because it has automated ammunition feed and is radar-directed has tremendous hitting power. That launcher may be provided with scores of multi-purpose missiles, anti-air, anti-ship or anti-submarine — perhaps even nuclear weapons. The development of vertical launch system (VLS) seems set to make warships appear even more underarmed when in fact enormous striking power will lurk below decks.

The pressure of volume criticality has forced warship designers to move weight upwards with high superstructures topped by multiple radar sensors. In turn to retain stability, this has meant the use of lightweight materials such as aluminium which itself burns once ignited at high temperatures. Modern warships are therefore 'soft' targets carrying very little armour and then just around critical installations such as missile magazines. Survivability, therefore, very largely depends on defensive weapons, both passive and active plus composite fleet operations of the kind outlined above with special purpose forces providing defence in depth.

This emphasis on the weapon system is critical if the surface warship is to survive, both as an effective fighting machine in the face of the air and sub-surface threat and in terms of cost with a single destroyer gobbling up vast chunks of any defence budget. The lessons of recent conflicts have proved however the surface warship still has a vital role to play.

Below: *Inside the operations centre of a Royal Navy warship. The pressure of space for control rooms and electronic systems is a critical design factor in small warships*

Right: *The Soviet cruiser Kirov, one of the biggest warships apart from aircraft carriers to be built since the end of the Second World War*

GLOSSARY

AAA:	Anti-aircraft artillery
AAM:	Air-to-air missile
ADV:	Air defence variant
AFCS:	Automatic flight control system
AFV:	Armoured fighting vehicle
AI:	Artificial intelligence
APC:	Armoured personnel carrier
APDS:	Armour-piercing discarding sabot
APFSDS:	Armour-piercing fin-stabilising discarding-sabot
ARM:	Anti-radiation missile
ASAT:	Anti-satellite
ASM:	Air-to-surface missile
ASTOVL:	Advanced short take-off/vertical landing
ATF:	Advanced tactical fighter
CEP:	Circular error of probability
CFC:	Carbon-fibre composite
COMSAT:	Communications satellite
C^{3}I:	Command, communications, control and intelligence
DEEC:	Digital electronic engine control
DFCS:	Digital flight control system
ECCM:	Electronic counter-countermeasure
EFA:	European fighter aircraft
EMP:	Electromagnetic pulse
ESM:	Electronic surveillance measures
ET:	Emerging technology
EW:	Electronic warfare
FLIR:	Forward-looking infra-red
FSW:	Forward-swept wing
GLCM:	Ground-launched cruise missile
HEAT:	High-explosive anti-tank
HEATFS:	High-explosive anti-tank fin-stabilised
HEP:	High-explosive plastic
HESH:	High-explosive squash-head
HVM:	Hyper-velocity missile
ICBM:	Intercontinental ballistic missile
IFFC:	Integrated flight/fire control
IFV:	Infantry fighting vehicle
INS:	Inertial navigation system
IR:	Infra-red
JAFE:	Joint advanced fighter engine
JTIDS:	Joint tactical information distribution system

LGB:	Laser-guided bombs
MAD:	Mutual assured destruction
MAW:	Mission-adaptive wing
MIRV:	Multiple independently targetable re-entry vehicle
MMW:	Millimetre-wave
NAS:	Numerical aerodynamic simulator (electronic windtunnel)
NBC:	Nuclear, biological and chemical
PBV:	Post boost vehicle
PCB:	Plenum-chamber burning
PELS:	Precision emitter location system
PGSM:	Precision-guided submunition
PLSS:	Precision location strike system
RAM:	Radar-absorbent material
RPV:	Remotely-piloted vehicle
SAM:	Surface-to-air missile
SIGINT:	Signals intelligence
SLBM:	Sea-launched ballistic missile
STOL:	Short-take-off-and-landing
STOVL:	Short take-off/vertical landing
TAV:	Trans-atmospheric vehicle
TNF:	Theatre nuclear force
USAF:	US Air Force
USB:	Upper surface blowing
UVS:	Unmanned vehicle system
VATOL:	Vertical attitude take-off and landing
VHSIC:	Very high-speed integrated circuits
VLSI:	Very large-scale integration.

INDEX

ACKNOWLEDGEMENTS

Campbell Rawkins and The Research House would like to thank all those organisations and individuals in aerospace and systems manufacturers, in government departments, in the services and in the press who have supplied the illustrations for this book.

Jacket: United States Air Force Title: Dassault-Breguet, Pages 6: McDonnell-Douglas, 7: USAF, 12: Thomson-CSF, 13: USAF: 14: US Navy, 16: Royal Air Force, 19: USAF, 19(below): US Navy, 20: Mitsubishi, 21: Grumman, 23: US Department of Defense, 23(top): USAF, 24: USAF, 29: McDonnell-Douglas, 29: McDonnell Douglas, 30: General Dynamics, 31: USAF, 34: Dassault-Breguet, 35: Saab-Scania, 36: Lockheed, 38: McDonnell-Douglas, 39: Rolls-Royce, 40: Lockheed, 40: USAF, 43: US DoD, 44: Matra, 44(below): McDonnell-Douglas, 45: USAF, 47: British Aerospace, 50: Hughes Aircraft, 51: MBB, 51(below): Hunting, 52: Oerlikon, 53: Vought, 54: Boeing, 55: Lockheed, 56: Frazer Nash, 57: ML Aviation 62: USAF, 63: USAF, 63(below): USAF, 66: USAF, 67: US Navy, 68: USAF, 69: USAF, 69(below): Martin Marietta, 70: US Navy, 71: US Navy, 72: USAF, 73(top): USAF, 73(below): US Navy, 77: Vought, 78: MoD, 79: Vought, 82-3: USAF, 86-7: BAe, 87: Hughes Aircraft, 88: Swedish Army, 88(below): US Army, 89: Bofors, 93: US DoD, 94: Mike Roberts, 95(top): US Army, 96: General Dynamics, 97: UK Land Forces, 98: Ford Aerospace, 102: GKN-Sankey, 103: Pilkington, 104: Chemring, 105: Krauss Maffei, 107: AMX, 109(top): US DoD, 109(below): Euromissile, 110: GKN-Sankey, 111: FMC Corp, 112: US Army, 113(top): US Army, 113: Thorn-EMI, 114(top): USAF, 114(below): Ford Aerospace, 115: Hughes Aircraft, 116: MBB, 117: Thyssen-Henschel, 120: US DoD, 121: Grumman, 122: NATO, 123: Westinghouse, 123(below): Westinghouse, 124: Chemring Ltd, 125: US Army, 126: Plessey, 127: USMC, 128: Grumman, 129(top): Westinghouse, 129(below): Grumman, 130: Bell Helicopter, 132: Electronnica SPA, 134: Hughes Aircraft, 135 (top): MBB, 135: Thyssen-Henschel, 142: NASA, 143: NASA, 145(both): USAF, 146: NASA, 147: Hughes Aircraft, 149: NASA, 150: Ford Aerospace, 151: USAF, 152: RCA, 155: Lockheed, 157: USAF, 160: Vickers, 161: Dassault-Breguet, 162: US Navy, 163: US DoD, 166: Thomson CSF, 167(top): Lockheed, 167(below): Westland Helicopters, 168: Thomson CSF, 169: Marconi, 170: US Navy, 171: Aerospatiale, 172: Aerospatiale, 174: McDonnell-Douglas, 175: US Navy

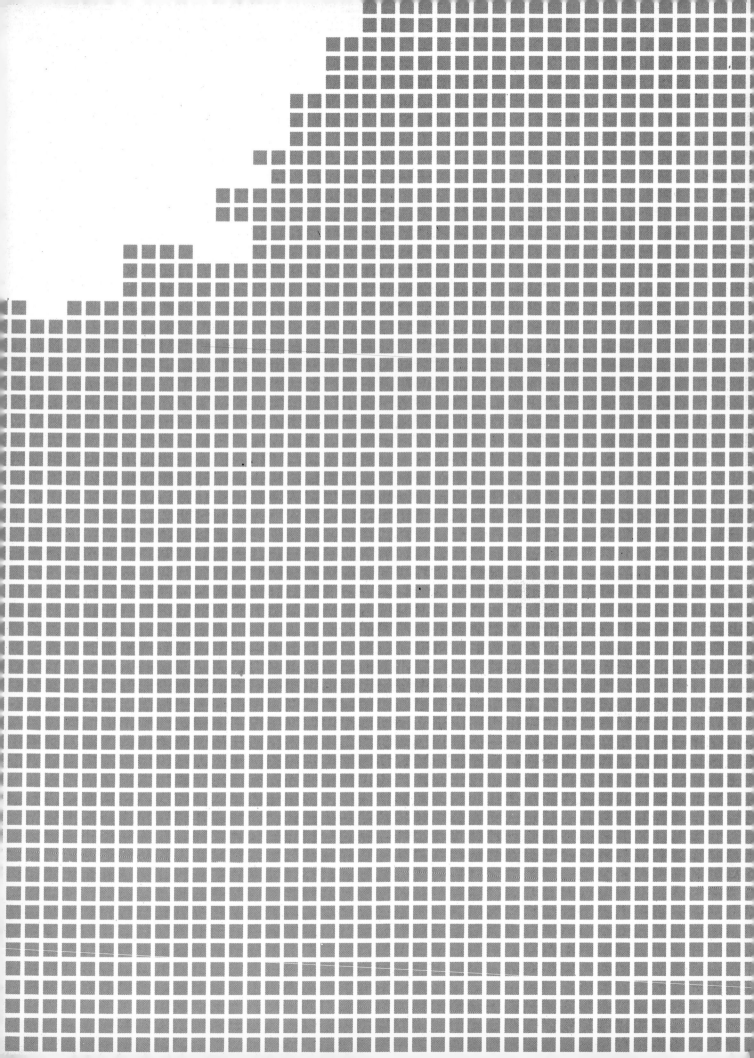